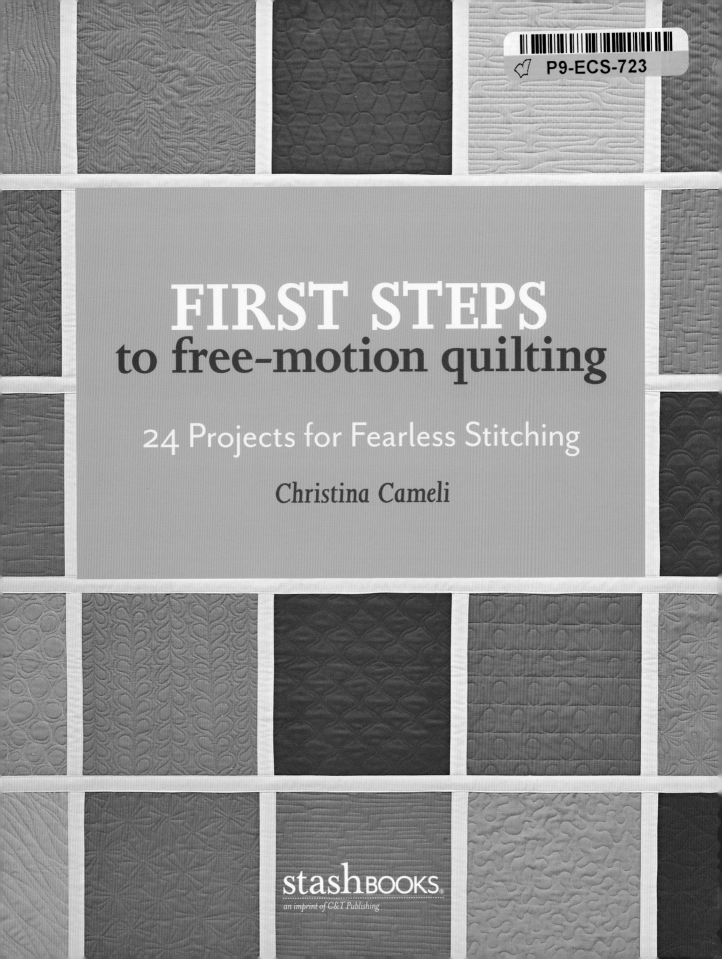

FIRST STEPS
to free-motion quilting

24 Projects for Fearless Stitching

Christina Cameli

stashBOOKS®

an imprint of C&T Publishing

Text copyright © 2013 by Christina Cameli

Photography and Artwork copyright © 2013 by C&T Publishing, Inc.

Publisher: Amy Marson

Creative Director: Gailen Runge

Art Director: Kristy Zacharias

Editor: S. Michele Fry

Technical Editors: Teresa Stroin and Amanda Siegfried

Book Designer: Michelle Thompson | Fold & Gather Design

Production Coordinator: Jenny Davis

Production Editor: Alice Mace Nakanishi

Illustrator: Valyrie Friedman

Photo Assistant: Mary Peyton Peppo

Photography by Christina Carty-Francis, Diane Pedersen, and Nissa Brehmer of C&T Publishing, Inc., unless otherwise noted

Published by Stash Books, an imprint of C&T Publishing, Inc., P.O. Box 1456, Lafayette, CA 94549

Library of Congress Cataloging-in-Publication Data

Cameli, Christina, 1976-

 First steps to free-motion quilting : 24 projects for fearless stitching / Christina Cameli.

   pages cm

 ISBN 978-1-60705-672-0 (soft cover)

1. Patchwork--Patterns. 2. Machine quilting--Patterns. I. Title.

 TT835.C35617 2013

 746.46--dc23

                    2012049279

Printed in China

10 9 8 7 6 5 4 3 2 1

Dedication

For Mary Ann Cameli

Acknowledgments

I can attest that a book appears only through much nurturing of the author. I have profound gratitude to so many people: to my family, for raising me as an artist and loving me as I am; to my friends, for sharing my joy; to my teachers, for passing on their wisdom; to my students, for choosing to grow; to my readers, for convincing me I had something to share; to my publisher and editors, for taking a chance with such enthusiasm; and most of all, to Charlton and Ellery, for more patience and love than I could imagine. Thank you all, from the bottom of my heart, for helping me share what needed to be shared.

Contents

Introduction

Do you feel a thrill at running your hand over stitching, or catch your breath at a beautiful design created with thread? If you delight in the look and feel of free-form stitching but have wondered how to get started, I wrote this book for you.

I want to get you excited about free-motion quilting. I want you to feel the joy of starting, the pleasure of overcoming obstacles, and the contentment of loving what you've made. I want you to be giddy when you present your next quilt to its recipient.

The basics of free-motion quilting are not at all difficult. The supplies needed are minimal, and with them you can stitch an endless array of designs to personalize your creations. You are not limited to straight lines or gentle curves; with thread you can draw any design you can imagine.

As many quilters are aware, the thing that will make or break success with free-motion stitching is *practice*. And that's where some of us get stuck. Do we risk practicing on a beautiful quilt top? Do we just stitch aimlessly on some scraps of fabric?

This book offers a different approach. I bet you sew because you love fabric and you love making beautiful things with it. So let's do that—make something beautiful *while* practicing free-motion stitching. Learn the basics, gather the supplies, and then pick a project and start stitching. The projects are designed to be light on assembly so you can spend most of your time actually stitching, improving your free-motion quilting skills.

I'm ready to help you over the little hiccups that keep people from free-motion quilting. If you're not sure what design to stitch on your next quilt, I've included a chapter of designs. If problems pop up, there's a troubleshooting guide.

This book won't turn you into an expert quilter; I'm not an expert quilter either. But you and I can still make beautiful things with needle and thread. It's simply a matter of jumping in with joy and getting better as you go. I love to share the magic of stitching this way.

Whether you've just discovered free-motion quilting or have wanted to try it for years, this book is your bridge, from wondering to knowing, from hesitating to acting. You're ready. Take a deep breath, get in there, and amaze yourself.

The Necessities

The good news is you probably already have most of the items you need for free-motion quilting: a machine, needles, and thread. Just gather a few more supplies and you'll be on your way!

YOU NEED A DARNING FOOT

Unlike other sewing you've done, free-motion quilting relies on *you* to move the fabric in the direction you want it to go, instead of having the machine do so. To allow free movement of your work, you need a darning foot, sometimes called a free-motion foot. This special sewing machine foot lets you move fabric in any direction between stitches, but keeps the fabric against the stitch plate when the needle is down to allow the stitch to form properly. Plastic or metal, square or round, closed or open, they all do the same job. Any darning foot that fits your machine should work. If you have more than one darning foot to choose from, choose the one that offers you better visibility. In other words, an open toe rather than a closed toe, offset shank versus inline, thinner versus thicker. Your local sewing machine dealer can help you find a darning foot that will fit your machine.

Variety of darning feet

YOU NEED A CLEAN MACHINE

During sewing, and particularly quilting, lint from the thread, the fabrics, and the batting will accumulate around the foot and under the stitch plate. Lint buildup can interfere with the action of the thread enough to cause thread breakage or skipped stitches. If you've never cleaned out your machine before, now is the time to learn.

Cleaning a sewing machine

Remove the bobbin and clean out the inside of the bobbin case. Lint in the corners of the bobbin case and housing can cause problems. Give a quick wipe to this area with every bobbin change.

Remove bobbin to clean out bobbin case and housing.

Next, remove the stitch plate (if it can be removed), using the owner's manual to guide you. This is usually done by releasing a lever or loosening screws. Use a soft brush or a scrap of batting to wipe away any clumps of lint accumulating around the feed dogs and bobbin housing. Do this full, plate-off cleanout every three or four bobbin changes. Oil the machine regularly as recommended in the owner's manual.

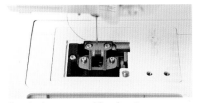
Stitch plate removed for cleaning

TIP
Cut batting scraps into 2" squares to use for lint cleanup.

Is your machine big enough?

Even though it can be tight, you *can* quilt bed-sized quilts on a regular home machine. Remember that you will only have to fit enough of the quilt under the sewing machine's arm to reach to the middle of the quilt (you can quilt the other half from the other side). So if you have a quilt 88" × 100", you only have to get 44" under the arm of the machine to be able to reach every area of the quilt for quilting. This is possible even on smaller home machines.

YOU NEED THE MACHINE'S EXTENSION TABLE

Many sewing machines have a free arm for detail sewing and a larger extension table that fits around the free arm. Trying to quilt on a skinny free arm is an exercise in frustration. If your machine doesn't have an extension table, try this test: Place your hands as shown in the picture below. If your palms and fingers are not supported, you'll need to put a table around the machine bed.

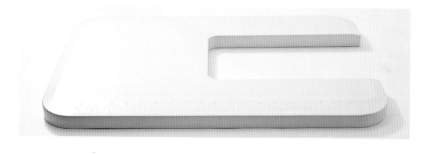

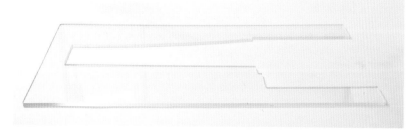

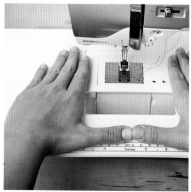

Palms and fingers are supported.

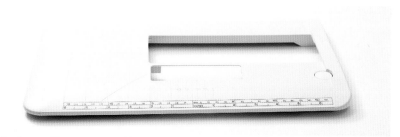

Sewing machine extension tables

If you need an extension table, you can order a custom Plexiglas extension table through your local sewing machine store. Alternatively, you can purchase a sewing table that a machine lowers into, so that the tabletop lies flush with the surface of the sewing machine. This creates a continuous flat surface and reduces the effort necessary to move the quilt top as you stitch.

YOU NEED TO ADJUST THE FEED DOGS

When a sewing machine moves the fabric for straight stitching, it does so with the feed dogs, which pull the fabric forward with every stitch. For free-motion stitching, you must stop the feed dogs from pulling on the fabric, so that you can guide the work in the direction you want it to go. If your machine has a lever or switch to lower the feed dogs, use it and you can move fabric freely. If not, there are other ways you can stop the feed dogs from interfering.

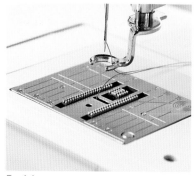

Feed dogs up

Feed dogs down

The simplest solution is simply setting the machine's stitch length to zero. At this setting, the feed dogs will go up and down, but they will not pull on the fabric. Some quilters prefer to stitch this way, even though their machines are able to lower the feed dogs. So if you can't lower the feed dogs on your machine, don't fret; just set the stitch length to zero!

If you prefer that the feed dogs not touch the fabric at all, you may cover them with an index card. Punch a hole in the middle for the needle to pass through. Tape all four edges of the index card to the machine to keep them from catching on your work. Instead of an index card, you may wish to try a specialty mat for free-motion quilting that adheres to the machine bed, covering the feed dogs while providing a smooth, slick surface to allow easy movement of the quilt.

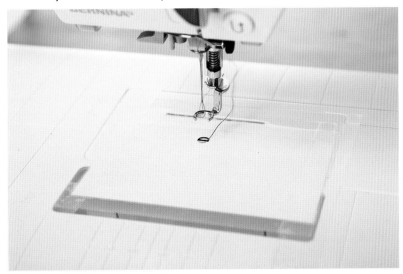

Index card covers feed dogs.

Alternatively, your machine may have a lever to raise the stitch plate *above* the feed dogs. I typically recommend against this approach because it will take up valuable space between the stitch plate and the darning foot, squishing the fabric and making it harder to move your work.

As another option, you may be able to purchase a feed dog cover for your machine that will snap to the stitch plate over the feed dogs. Experiment and see what works best for you.

YOU NEED A SHARP NEEDLE

Old needles don't work well for free-motion quilting. A dull or slightly bent needle will soon result in skipped stitches or broken threads. Start quilting with a nice sharp needle. Most machines will work well with either universal needles or quilting needles. Quilting needles are a little sharper than universal needles.

Some needles that can be used for free-motion quilting

The numbers on the needle package refer to the size of the needle in the sizing systems of Europe and the United States. The larger the number, the larger the size of the needle and its eye. Use larger needles for thicker threads. I recommend universal 80/12 or quilting 90/14 needles to start.

Replace needles after about eight hours of stitching, or when thread or stitch problems tell you to do so. Sometimes a different size or type of needle is called for to deal with a specific machine problem. See Troubleshooting (page 139) if you think you may need a different needle.

YOU NEED QUALITY THREAD

Many threads work well for free-motion quilting. Cotton, polyester, and silk in a variety of thicknesses are commonly used. Thread thickness is frequently described using a weight system. The larger the number of the thread weight, the *thinner* the thread, and the subtler the stitching will appear. The smaller the number, the *thicker* the thread, and the more visible each stitch will be. Most of the projects in this book were stitched with 40- and 50-weight threads.

Aurifil 28/2 cotton

Aurifil 40/2 cotton

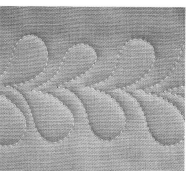
So Fine 50/3 polyester

The Bottom Line 60/2 polyester

YLI silk #100 2-ply

Some threads that can be used for free-motion quilting

TIP
Thread weights are often given along with the number of yarns in the thread. For example, a 40-weight, 3-ply thread is generally indicated as 40/3. Some quilting threads, however, are described with a number sign (#) before the number. This is not always the same as the thread weight. The best way to understand how a thread will appear on a quilt is to stitch a test sample.

It is fine to start with whatever thread you have at home. However, free-motion stitching puts a lot of stress on thread, so threads that you normally use may not perform as well as you expect under these circumstances. Try new threads if you encounter problems or get curious. Over time and with experimentation, you'll eventually land on a favorite thread for both your stitching style and your machine's particular temperament. I have great luck with both Aurifil and Superior threads for their strength and the minimal lint they produce while quilting.

For most projects, I recommend using the same thread in the top and bobbin. Some machines work best when the top and bobbin threads are the same weight. However, many quilters use different threads in the top and bobbin without difficulty. Some quilters prefer to use a very fine specialty thread in the bobbin.

YOU NEED FABRIC

Quilting-weight cottons and linen are used for most of the projects in this book. If you are just starting free-motion quilting, try to avoid fabrics such as denim or batiks, which can present special challenges. If you do use batiks, be sure to prewash them to remove any residual wax from the fabric.

YOU NEED BATTING

For quilts and quilted projects, the choice of batting will affect the free-motion quilting results. In general, low-loft battings are ideal for free-motion quilting. Cotton, polyester, wool, bamboo, and silk are all used with success by free-motion quilters. Avoid any batting you could describe as puffy.

Low-loft battings

YOU NEED BASTING PINS

To hold quilt layers together and keep them from shifting and puckering as you quilt, you should temporarily baste them together. I baste my work with curved basting pins, which are widely available and can be reused. For instructions, see Layering and Basting Quilts and Projects (page 137). Some quilters prefer to spray baste their quilts, and this method typically works just fine for free-motion quilting. Feel free to try this approach.

Curved basting pins

YOU NEED QUILTING GLOVES

Quilting gloves are available in different sizes and have a textured surface to increase traction on fabric. They give you better control over the quilt than bare hands and keep your hands from becoming fatigued as quickly. Gloves are a small investment and will last for years. My favorites have small grippy dots on them that provide traction on both the palms and the fingers. Some quilters cut off one or two fingertips of their gloves to make needle threading and pin removal easier.

Gloves for quilting

As alternatives to quilting gloves, some quilters prefer latex gloves, gardening gloves, industrial glove liners, or rubber office fingertips. Others prefer to grasp their quilts with well-moisturized bare hands. I encourage new quilters to start with quilting gloves but try alternatives if they feel uncomfortable with the hold they have on the quilt.

YOU NEED A PLACE TO SKETCH

In a way, free-motion quilting is drawing with thread. Sketching, therefore, is a great way to practice. I recommend dedicating a big blank journal for sketching quilting designs. Use this journal to get you used to creating continuous-line designs. Put the pen down and see what patterns you can create without lifting the pen from the page. Try variations on a theme. How many designs can you doodle with spirals in them, for example?

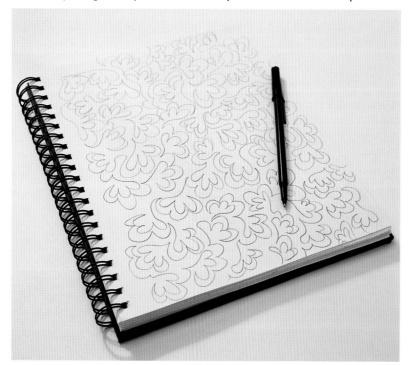

TIP
Sketch new designs in your journal whenever they present themselves, and the journal will soon become an invaluable design library in addition to being a tool for experimentation and practice.

YOU NEED A POSITIVE ATTITUDE!

Doing something you've never done before? That's an adventure! So go in with curiosity and excitement. See what happens. Remember to be kind to yourself. New skills take time. You've learned other challenging skills over the course of your life, and you'll certainly learn this one, too.

TIP
You're not drawing, just doodling. This journal is for your eyes only— go wild!

When you have a project to stitch, let your journal help you. Before quilting a new design, fill a few pages of the journal with it. Working on paper helps you get a feel for how the design flows and where the twists and turns come. It's much cheaper and easier to work these things out on paper than on fabric.

Some quilters prefer to save paper by practicing their sketches on a dry erase board. Others use old phone books and markers. Some doodle during meetings on bits of scrap paper—whatever works for you. Don't underestimate the benefit of sketching for improving eye-hand coordination and familiarity with quilting designs.

The Basics

Sitting down to stitch for the first time is embarking on a journey. Free-motion quilting asks a bit more of you and your machine than typical sewing. Take challenges a step at a time and get to know your sewing machine better than you ever have before. If needed, consult Troubleshooting (page 139).

START-UP CHECKLIST

Go through this checklist each time you start quilting.

- ☐ Clean machine
- ☐ Extension table
- ☐ Darning foot
- ☐ Fresh needle
- ☐ Feed dogs down or covered (*optional*)
- ☐ Quilting thread
- ☐ Quilting gloves
- ☐ Set machine for straight stitch
- ☐ Adjust the machine stitch length and width to zero, or as low as they will go.

Now let's start quilting!

MAKING A PRACTICE PAD

Before you start stitching on a project, do some warm-up stitching on a practice pad. Cut two pieces of fabric and a piece of batting to create a mini quilt sandwich about 12″ × 18″. Baste it with pins about every 5″.

GETTING A HOLD ON THE QUILT

I have experimented with different quilt holds, and the one I always come back to is the U shape. This hold allows me to move the quilt with precision and keeps puckers from developing as I stitch.

The U shape

Place your hands on the quilt top a comfortable distance apart, with your thumbs extended toward each other, so that the thumbs and forefingers create a U shape. The tips of your fingers and thumbs rest on the quilt, as well as the outside edge of the palms. The rest of the palm is lifted somewhat off the quilt top, in a relaxed position. This creates much less hand stress than trying to keep the entire hand flat on the quilt. Use a slight downward and outward pressure with your hands to keep the area you are stitching flat, preventing wrinkles. While a number of quilting hoops are marketed to free-motion quilters, I think no quilting hoop is more adaptable or easier to use than your own hands!

Keep your hands closer in for intricate work and place them farther out when quilting larger designs. You will have good control of the quilt within the U, but control will deteriorate as you stitch outside its boundaries. Stop and reposition your hands as you go, keeping the needle within the U.

TIP

Some quilters prefer grabbing their quilts with one or both hands. Feel free to try different holds on the quilt if the U is not working for you.

STARTING AND STOPPING

1. Place the quilt under the machine and lower the presser foot.

2. Take a stitch into the quilt and then bring the needle back up to its highest point.

3. Tug lightly on the tail of the top thread until you can see a loop of the bobbin thread come up through the quilt. *(See Figure A.)* Pull this loop gently until you have brought the entire tail of the bobbin thread up to the top.

4. Reposition so the needle is directly over the place where you took the first stitch. *(See Figure B.)*

5. Place one hand on the quilt. Hold the thread tails back with the other hand. Lock the first stitches by taking a few tiny stitches forward and backward over one another. You are securing the threads in place to keep them from unraveling over time. If you prefer, you can just take a few stitches in place to secure the threads. *(See Figure C.)*

6. Place your hands on the quilt in the U shape and begin stitching the design. Guide the quilt with your hands while you press the pedal. Keep your hands on the quilt in the U shape. Trim the thread ends as needed to keep from stitching over them. *(See Figure D.)*

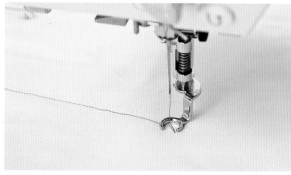

A. Pulling thread loop up

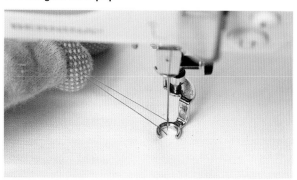

B. Needle repositioned

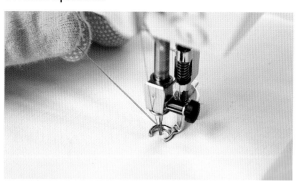

C. Locking the stitches

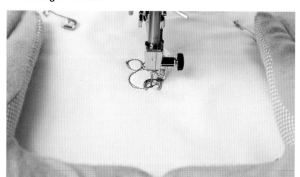

D. Beginning stitching

7. When the stitching needs to go beyond the U *(See Figure E.)*, stop stitching and reposition your hands *(See Figure F.)*. Some machines have a needle-down feature that stops the needle in the down position. This makes repositioning faster; if the needle is down in the fabric you are free to reposition your hands without worrying that the quilt will shift. If the needle stops in the up position, move your hands one at a time to keep the quilt in place while you reposition your hands. Or use the hand wheel to put the needle down so that you are free to remove both hands from the quilt.

8. If you have a basting pin within the U, remove it when you reposition your hands; then you are free to stitch within the entire area. *(See Figure G.)*

9. Continue in this way: stitch, reposition, stitch. Readjust the quilt as needed so it does not catch on the corners of the table.

10. When you are ready to stop, lock the stitches as you did at the beginning, by taking a few small stitches back and forth over one another. Pull the quilt out and clip the threads close to the quilt top.

TIP
Starts and stops are not as secure as continuous stitching, so try to plan the quilting for as few stops and starts as possible.

E. Stitching has reached edge of U.

F. Hands repositioned.

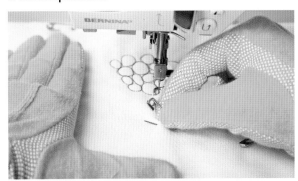

G. Remove basting pins as you come to them.

THE ESSENTIAL STEPS

Take a single stitch at the starting point.
Pull the bobbin thread up.
Lock the beginning stitches.
Stitch, reposition hands, stitch, reposition ...
Lock the end stitches.

YOUR FIRST STITCHING SESSION

If you've never free-motion quilted, do the following exercises on a practice pad (see Making a Practice Pad, page 11) to test the tension settings and get the feel of moving the quilt as you stitch.

1. Stitch some close-set lines up and down from the top to the bottom of the practice pad. Start the first line at the top right of the practice pad and stitch a line downward by pushing the quilt away from you. Stop and reposition your hands as needed. At the bottom, stitch a bit to the left (by moving the practice pad to the right) and stitch the next line up, by pulling the quilt top back toward you.

- -

TIP

You do not need to turn the quilt; you simply change the direction you are moving it with your hands. The top of the quilt sandwich should stay at the top and the bottom should stay at the bottom as you work.

- -

After you've made ten or so lines, stop and look at the back. If you see loops of the top thread on the back of the quilt, increase the top thread tension by a notch.

2. Try making some zigzags from top to bottom by moving your hands from side to side while pushing the quilt away from you. Check the back again. If loops of the top thread are coming to the back at the points, increase the top tension a bit more.

3. Try making some loops by moving your hands in a swooping motion. Again, you don't need to turn the quilt. Check the back one more time. Hopefully you are seeing only bobbin thread on the bottom and only top thread on top. If the top thread is pulling to the back on the curves, you may need to increase the top tension a bit. However, if the thread only pulls to the back when the stitches become very long, this is normal and will improve with practice as you achieve a more consistent stitch length. *(See Figure H.)*

4. Now fill up the remaining space on the practice pad with any patterns that appeal to you.

- -

TIP

It is a good idea to stitch some zigzags and loops on a practice pad whenever you start a project, switch threads, or change tension settings. This practice will help you discover and fix problems before you start stitching on a real quilt top, saving you from needing to rip out stitches.

- -

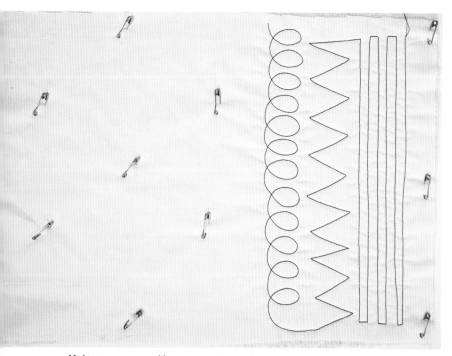

H. Lines, zigzags, and loops on practice pad

TENSION ADJUSTMENT

The top and bobbin threads each have adjustable tension. The tension of one thread affects the other thread's behavior. If the tension is out of balance, you will see one thread being pulled to the other side by the thread with the higher tension. Tension may need adjustment depending on the thickness of the item you are stitching and the thickness of the threads being used.

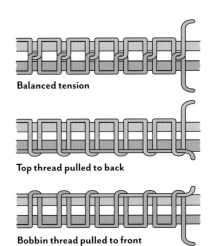

Balanced tension

Top thread pulled to back

Bobbin thread pulled to front

How should you adjust the tension?

If the top thread is being pulled to the back

Top (red) thread being pulled to back. Bobbin thread is not being pulled into quilt sandwich; it is just lying on back of quilt.

Increase the top thread tension (turn dial to the right, or to a higher number if the tension dial uses numbers) or decrease the bobbin thread tension (turn the bobbin tension screw counterclockwise).

If the bobbin thread is being pulled to the top

Bobbin (blue) thread being pulled to top. Top thread is not being pulled into quilt sandwich; it is just lying on top of quilt.

Decrease the top thread tension (turn dial to the left, or to a lower number if the tension dial uses numbers) or increase the bobbin thread tension (turn the bobbin tension screw clockwise).

Most of the time, only the top thread tension will need adjustment. However, I sometimes encounter machines whose bobbin tension needs adjusting as well. You are qualified to do this! Use the sewing machine manual to identify the bobbin tension adjustment screw. Mark the original setting of the screw by making a dot with a permanent marker, so you can return the tension screw to its original setting if needed. Make only a small turn at a time, equivalent to five minutes if the screw were the face of a clock. Test on a practice pad after each adjustment until you have solved the problem.

STITCHUS INTERRUPTUS

When the thread breaks or the bobbin runs out, you'll need to restart the stitching and secure the broken line of stitches. Restart the same way you did initially, placing the first few new stitches over the last few stitches you took before the thread ran out. This secures both sets of threads at the same time.

COMFORT WHILE STITCHING

Stay aligned with the machine. Sit directly in front of the needle, not off to the side. Some people stitch better with the chair raised or with a pillow on the chair. Try this if your elbows dip below the level of the extension table or if you are feeling arm fatigue as you stitch.

Keep shoulders relaxed and elbows down. They may rise as you work; consciously lower them.

Keep breathing as you stitch. If you're feeling anxious as you work, it's probably a sign that you're holding your breath. While working on a practice pad, be mindful of your breathing as you stitch, so breathing becomes part of your rhythm as well. Your mind and body work better with oxygen!

If you find yourself getting overly frustrated, stop and make sure you've met your basic needs for sleep, bathroom, food, and water. There's no point in torturing yourself at the sewing machine. Step away for an hour to care for yourself, or come back fresh tomorrow.

LOOK AHEAD OF THE NEEDLE

Get in the habit of looking an inch or two ahead of the needle when you quilt. Focus your eyes on the next spot you want to hit, and when you reach that spot, let your eyes flick ahead to the next target. Keeping your eyes off the needle allows you to see landmarks as you approach them and helps you guide the stitching more easily.

SMOOTH STARTS AND STOPS

It can be challenging to keep the stitching smooth when you restart after stopping to reposition your hands. You'll get better with practice. Restart at a slow speed and make sure you are not battling the weight of the quilt as you do. Some quilters do better if they raise the needle out of the quilt sandwich before they restart stitching.

SPEED AND STITCH LENGTH

A big part of getting the feel for free-motion quilting is learning to quilt a consistent number of stitches per inch. Don't drive yourself crazy measuring with a tape measure. Most quilters know what looks right, and that is usually from eight to twelve stitches per inch. Closer to four and you will have giant, loose, jagged stitches that are likely to catch on something and break. Closer to twenty and the stitches will pile up, looking thick and shaky.

Stitch length is a result of the speed at which you stitch and the pace at which you move the fabric. Stitching too slowly or moving the fabric too rapidly will create long stitches. Stitching too fast or moving your hands too slowly makes for teeny stitches. Practice will help you get a feel for moving your hands in sync with the stitching speed. This is a sort of intimacy that you develop with your machine through time.

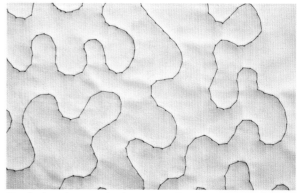

Result of stitching too slowly or moving hands too fast

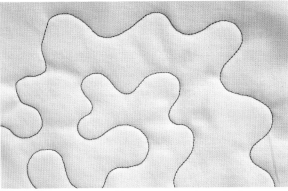

Result of stitching too quickly or moving hands too slowly

Start stitching at a medium speed. If you break a needle, try moving your hands more slowly. If the stitching is jagged and the stitches are large, try stitching faster. I find that people's stitching is generally more fluid when the machine is stitching at a moderately fast speed. However, if you start to feel out of control, take your foot off the pedal and then start again at a slower speed. It's normal to see wild inconsistencies in the stitch length at first. Keep on stitching; it will improve.

- -

TIP

Adjust your stitching speed to the task at hand. For more detailed work, stitch more slowly. For larger, less detailed designs, try stitching faster.

- -

PRACTICE, PRACTICE, AND PRACTICE

If your fairy godmother doesn't drop by tonight to turn you into an expert quilter, try plan B—practice. That's what this book is really about; pick a project that appeals to you and try it! Jumping in is the best way to learn.

MY TOP TEN FREE-MOTION QUILTING TIPS

1. Use a fresh, sharp needle.

2. Warm up on a practice pad.

3. Stop worrying; start stitching.

4. Keep breathing.

5. Look ahead of the needle.

6. Let your shoulders and elbows relax.

7. See what happens if you stitch a little faster.

8. If you feel out of control, stop, breathe, and then start again.

9. Don't be afraid to experiment.

10. Keep practicing; you're getting better every time!

Quilting Tips and Techniques

Now that you've absorbed the basics, you're ready to start stitching.
But if you'd like a few more tips to refine your quilting, read on!

SET YOURSELF UP FOR SUCCESS

If you're feeling worried about how the stitching will look on the finished project, choose a thread that blends well with the fabrics. If you have multiple fabrics to match, choose a thread to match the lighter fabrics—it will stand out less than a darker thread. Avoid stitching with dark threads on light fabrics.

Choose a lighter-weight thread (50-weight or higher), which will produce subtler stitching. Consider an organic quilting design, in which wobbles and irregularity can be part of the charm. Stitching is more obvious on solid fabrics, so consider prints if you're feeling less confident.

To get an idea of how the thread will look on the piece, unwind and lay a few loops of thread on the piece you will be quilting. Make sure to evaluate how the thread looks on top of the darkest and lightest fabrics.

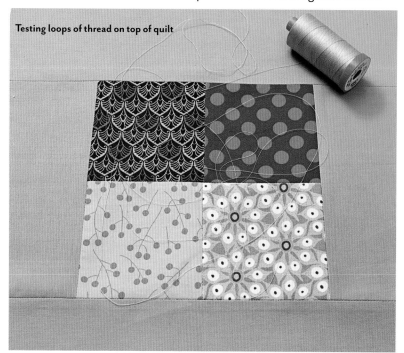

Testing loops of thread on top of quilt

FITTING A QUILT UNDER THE MACHINE ARM

When you have a large amount of the quilt to fit under the arm of your home sewing machine, you can either stuff or roll.

Rolling keeps the corners of the quilt out of the way and can provide a convenient place for grasping the quilt, but large rolls can be stiff and unwieldy, like a log. However, rolling can help a very large quilt fit into a very small space.

Stuffing the quilt unrolled will allow freer movement but also requires vigilance to keep corners and folds from getting under the portion of the quilt being stitched. It's terribly frustrating to realize you just stitched the quilt to itself! Remember that you only need to get half of the quilt under the machine arm to stitch to the middle, and the remainder can be quilted from the other side.

MAKING A FLAT AND SLIPPERY QUILTING SURFACE

The work surface should be as flat and smooth as possible to allow you to move the quilt evenly and with minimum effort. You can make an extension table more slippery with a specialty silicone or Teflon mat for the machine bed that lies over the extension table and allows the fabric to slide more easily over it. Alternatively, you can wipe the extension table with a silicone spray or rub it with waxed paper to make it slicker.

Silicone quilter's mat

Try to arrange as much room as you can to the left of the machine and behind it. This space will support the part of the quilt that is not under the machine arm, to keep it from hanging off the table and putting stress on your work area. A small table to the left of your chair can be useful as well for supporting any quilt bulk in front of the machine. As the quilt gathers in front of the machine you can even use your body to support it. Let the quilt lie against your chest and upper arms instead of hanging down toward your lap.

SEEING WHERE YOU'RE GOING

It's much easier to stitch when you can see what you're doing! Adequate lighting will keep you from having to crane your neck to see where you're stitching. You may need to add a lamp near the sewing machine. Also, when possible, keep the area you've already stitched in front of the machine and the ones you haven't stitched behind the machine, so you can more easily avoid quilting into areas you've already done. To do this, start with the bulk of the quilt behind the machine and stitch as you pull the quilt toward you.

PLANNING THE QUILTING ACROSS THE QUILT TOP

Facing a big quilt can be a little daunting. Go in with a plan.

I usually break up the quilt into rough sections and decide on an order for quilting them. I choose the sections based on the size of the quilt and the design I want to stitch. I start with the center areas whenever

possible. This allows any fullness of the quilt to be pushed outward as I go, making puckers less likely. I also appreciate finishing the hardest part while I am fresh and full of energy. It's all downhill from there! I work in a counter-clockwise direction around the quilt's perimeter when I can, which aids in visibility.

5	4	3
6	1	2
7	8	9

16	15	14	13
5	4	3	12
6	1	2	11
7	8	9	10

If I'm stitching a directional design such as stretchy meandering, I generally work in large columns or rows. Again, I start with the center column and work outward.

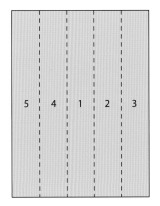

BECOMING A QUICK-CHANGE ARTIST

A number of the projects in this book require switching from free-motion to straight-line or zigzag stitching and back again. To make switching between machine functions as fast as possible, I keep a small bowl handy, such as one of the *Little Bowls* (page 78), next to my sewing machine. Whatever sewing foot I am not using waits in the bowl, so I always know where to find it. If your machine requires a screwdriver to switch feet, keep this handy as well. With your machine feet at the ready, switching feet and machine settings should take less than a minute.

MAKING THINGS POP OR RECEDE

The areas you quilt will push slightly back and away from the eye, and the areas that remain unquilted will seem to pop forward. This effect can add interesting dimension to your work. If you have a small area you want to emphasize, quilt the surrounding areas and leave the emphasis area unquilted.

Circles are left unquilted for added dimension.

QUILTING DENSELY VERSUS OPENLY

Denser quilting tends to stiffen a quilt and keep it from draping as freely as a more openly stitched quilt. Test looser and tighter versions of the design on a practice pad and see what feels best when you run your hand over it or hold it up to your face. If a quilt is intended for snuggling, consider quilting the designs on a larger scale to avoid ending up with a stiff quilt.

The quilt will contract more in areas of denser stitching. Try to keep the density of the stitching even across the quilt top. Stop occasionally and hold the area you started with up to the area you are working on to make sure the quilting is not loosening or tightening as you go.

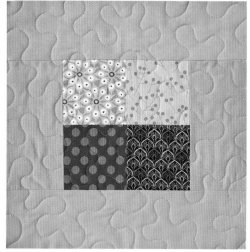

Looser quilting

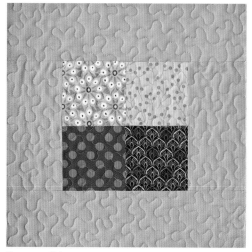

Denser quilting

CREATING REGULARLY SPACED DESIGNS

Use a guide to help you with stitching a regular design. The guide can be marks made with a fabric marker or pencil, pins placed at regular intervals (place them so you can stitch around them when possible), or my favorite, a piece of painter's masking tape.

Mark a piece of tape at the intervals where you want the design to repeat. Place it on the quilt top, making sure it is straight and level. Use the marks on the tape as landmarks for the repeating design, being careful not to stitch into the tape itself. Reposition this piece of tape with each new row, or as needed.

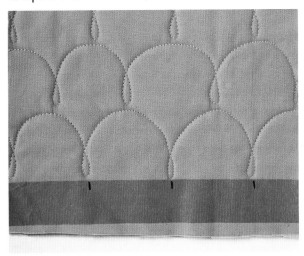

TIP
You can use a piece of tape, unmarked, to keep a linear design straight and level across a quilt top.

ENVISIONING THE QUILTING PATTERN

It can be difficult to envision a quilting design on a quilt. If you need to see it before you commit, try one of these tactics.

Take a digital photo of the quilt (or a portion of the quilt) and print it out on regular printer paper. Sketch the design you are envisioning over the picture. Print a few copies to compare different quilting designs.

Sketching quilting design on picture of quilt top

Use a sketching program on a computer to draw possible quilting designs over the digital photo of the quilt. This works best with touch-responsive screens or drawing pads, but if you have the technology, it can save you ink and paper!

For a technology-free option, lay a piece of clear vinyl over a portion of the quilt top. (Quilter's Vinyl from C&T Publishing works well for this.) Sketch the quilting design on the vinyl with an erasable marker. Be very sure to keep the marker away from the edges and avoid smudging the ink onto your hands or the quilt.

IF YOUR QUILTY SENSE IS TINGLING

When the machine suddenly sounds or feels different as you stitch, *stop* and check the back of your work to make sure you aren't missing a problem. Nothing is more disheartening than having to spend an entire hour ripping out a few minutes of stitching.

When you get the sensation that the quilt is starting to catch at the corners of the machine, or becoming harder to move, *stop*. Adjust the quilt so that it can move freely around the machine. Fluff out the corners to keep them from binding. You'll probably need to do this frequently when stitching a large allover design.

SHOULD YOU RIP IT OUT?

No one's quilting is perfect. So when the quilting doesn't go as you expect, should you take out the offending stitches and try again or just keep on stitching?

If you have a tension disaster, definitely take out the stitches and redo them. Loose loops of thread will not hold up over time. For the more common occurrence, where the tension is fine but the stitching just didn't go where it should have, decide whether it's a Big Mistake or a Little Inconsistency.

Big Mistakes draw attention to themselves. Nonquilters can point them out. You can find them immediately even after stepping away from the quilt top for a bit. They hurt to look at. Go ahead and take these out so they stop tormenting you.

Little Inconsistencies are things that blend in to the overall pattern on the quilt top after you step back. You stitched a wonky spiral or a wobbly leaf? The meandering crossed its own path or you worked yourself into the corner and had to stop and start over again somewhere else? These things happen to everyone. Nonquilters don't notice them, and it may take a minute of searching to find them again yourself after you step away for a while. Leave these Little Inconsistencies in. You will get better from *stitching*, not from taking out stitches. Take all the time you just saved by leaving those stitches in, and go stitch something else!

You'll probably notice Little Inconsistencies in this book. I left them in because I never would have completed a book if I thought my stitching had to be perfect. Consider them a loving reminder that imperfect stitching can still be beautiful.

THINGS THAT KEEP ME CALM ABOUT LITTLE INCONSISTENCIES

No one's going to notice anyway.

Done is better than perfect.

Everything looks better after you wash it.

MISTAKES I HOPE YOU DON'T MAKE

In the hopes that you can avoid some mistakes, here's a list of frustrating things I've done to myself.

Stitching the corner of the quilt to itself   When you are stitching near the edges of the quilt, make sure you can see the edges and corners of the backing fabric so you know they are not folded beneath the area you are working on. You may want to bring each corner of the backing fabric around to the top of the batting and hold it in place with a basting pin to make it less likely that the backing can be turned under as you work.

Stitching the edge of the quilt to the darning foot   If you stitch off the edge of the quilt top, come back onto it slowly, making sure the darning foot goes over rather than under the quilt top. If you do happen to stitch the quilt top over the darning foot, remove the darning foot from the machine so that you can remove the quilt, and then rip out the stitches from the back.

Stitching so close to a pin that it can't be removed   It's so tempting to want to stitch right up against a pin instead of removing it. But it's terribly inconvenient to find the darning foot trapped against a pin you stitched too close to. When this happens you'll have to break the thread, remove the pin, and restart the stitching. Make sure to remove any pin that is in the stitching area, or at least those within an inch or two of where you are stitching.

Not tightening the darn—I mean *darning*—foot tight enough   The strong vibrations of free-motion quilting can loosen a screw to the point that the darning foot comes off the machine as you stitch. This can be loud and scary. It will probably break a needle and it may require the machine to be serviced. If your machine uses a screw to attach the darning foot, make sure it's on tight!

Stitching a glove to the quilt   Yes, this means I let the needle get way too close to my finger and attached the glove to the quilt. Make yourself stop and reposition when the stitching approaches your hands. This will save you from having to remove the glove (or worse, blood!) from the quilt.

KEEP LEARNING

So many skilled teachers are sharing their free-motion quilting skills. Seek them out! Buy their books, read their blogs, go to their classes. Learn from them. You never know whose tip or process will click for you and make your quilting that much better. Just keep in mind that you will get better from *quilting*. You know the basics now, and that's all you need to start. Don't spend all your time on theory at the expense of practice. The practice is where all the fun is!

Quilting Designs

I've sketched basic continuous-line quilting designs and their simple variations in this chapter. These designs are meant to be stitched freehand, without marking the design on the quilt top. Practice the designs by tracing them with your finger or sketching them with pen and paper. Sketch the design without lifting the pen. You will find that some designs require retracing along a previously stitched line to get to an open space. This will quickly become second nature.

The designs are grouped into families that are formed the same way. Each form is infinitely variable. You will discover your own versions and combinations as you develop your unique quilting style. I hope you find lots of inspiration in the pages that follow.

EDGE-TO-EDGE LINES

These designs are formed with lines that go from one edge of the piece to the other, sometimes touching or overlapping one another. For tips on stitching designs with regular spacing, see Creating Regularly Spaced Designs (page 21).

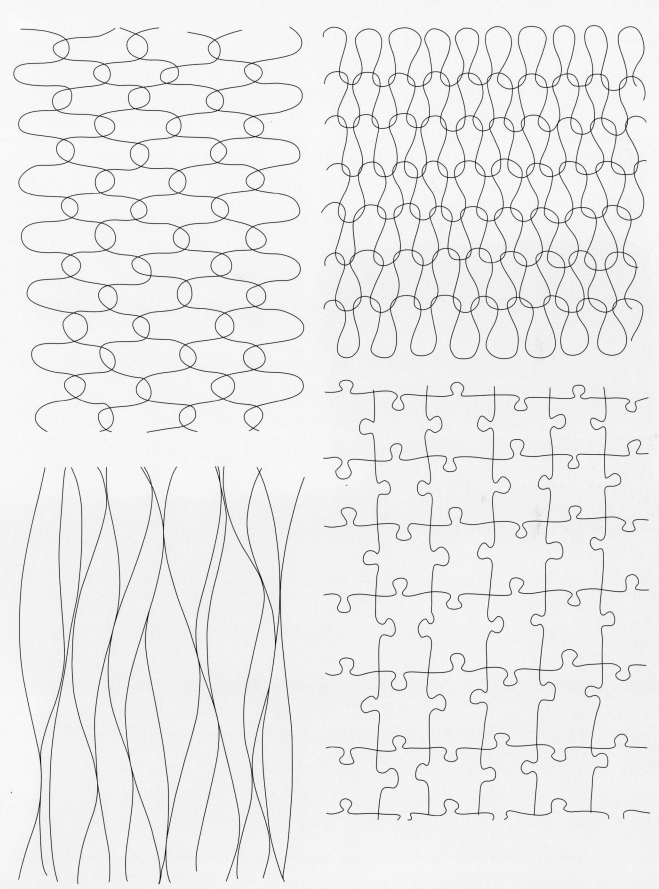

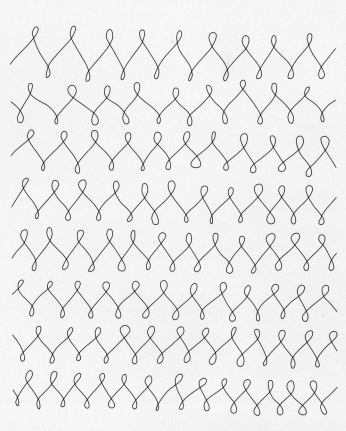

PEBBLES

Pebbles are simply a bunch of circles nestled up against one another. One pebble is formed, and then the next one is stitched right next to it. Travel around a pebble, overstitching when necessary, to get to an open space for starting the next pebble. Change the shape of a pebble or add a motif inside it for variety.

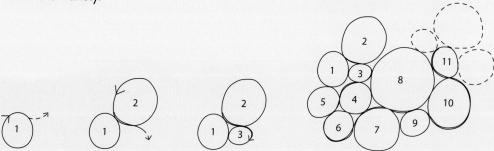

How to form pebbles: From a completed pebble you can choose any of several places to start the next pebble.

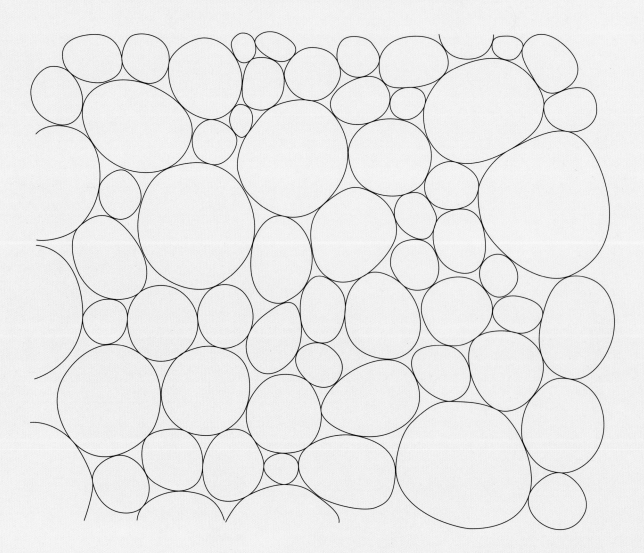

KISSING

With these designs, each motif kisses the next at a single point. When one motif is completed, you stitch along the lines of that motif to get to a starting point for the next one. It is similar to pebbling, only with more complex shapes.

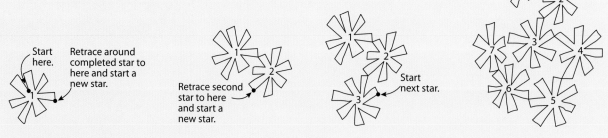

How to form kissing designs

MEANDERING

Meandering generally means a wiggly line that goes in all directions without a clear pattern and without crossing its own path. Many quilters like to think of puzzle pieces or gingerbread men as they stitch a meandering pattern.

The key to meandering is for the line to switch directions frequently. If you find yourself getting into a long wiggle that won't stop, use a two- or three-lump unit like the ones below to get you going in a new direction.

Two- and three-lump units for changing direction of long wiggles

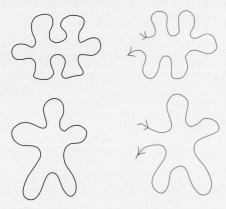

Meandering shapes inspired by puzzle pieces and gingerbread men

When meandering, you will work in blob-like areas. The edges of the areas you stitch do not need to be straight. In fact, it's better if they undulate a bit so that when you come back and stitch the adjacent section, the new line of stitching can nestle into the little nooks and crannies of the previously stitched area. Notice how the meandering proceeds up, down, and across in the illustration below, and how each section (shown in a different color) is stitched in a blob shape instead of a squared-off area. Developing smooth, consistent meandering takes practice. Don't get discouraged; just keep stitching!

Below are some meandering variations. I have included some designs that cross the stitching path. Even though they aren't strictly meandering, they do proceed in a meandering fashion.

STRETCHY MEANDERING

Meandering designs can be stretched out into a directional pattern. Where the lines change direction, you can add points, spirals, or flame licks for different effects.

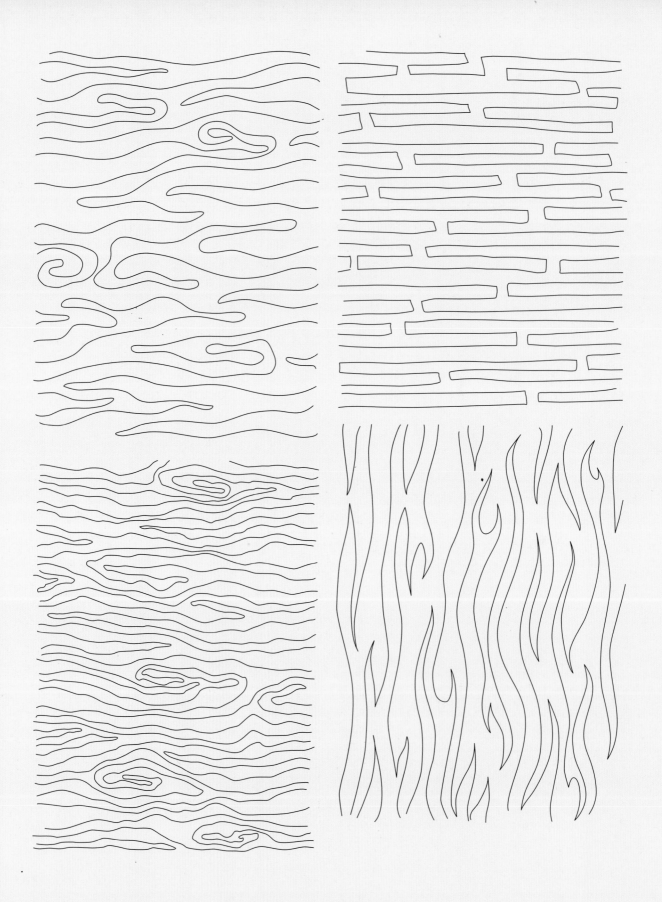

SPIRALS

Spirals are simple and lovely in lines or as an allover design. Be sure to leave room to get back out of the spiral.

ECHOING PATTERNS

With these patterns, a shape is stitched and then echoed one or more times. New motifs emerge beside or between previously stitched motifs. A classic echoing design is the paisley pattern.

How to form paisley pattern

SCALLOPS

Simple arcs look so elegant in a repeating pattern, and intersecting arcs can be very grand indeed. Be sure to see Creating Regularly Spaced Designs (page 21).

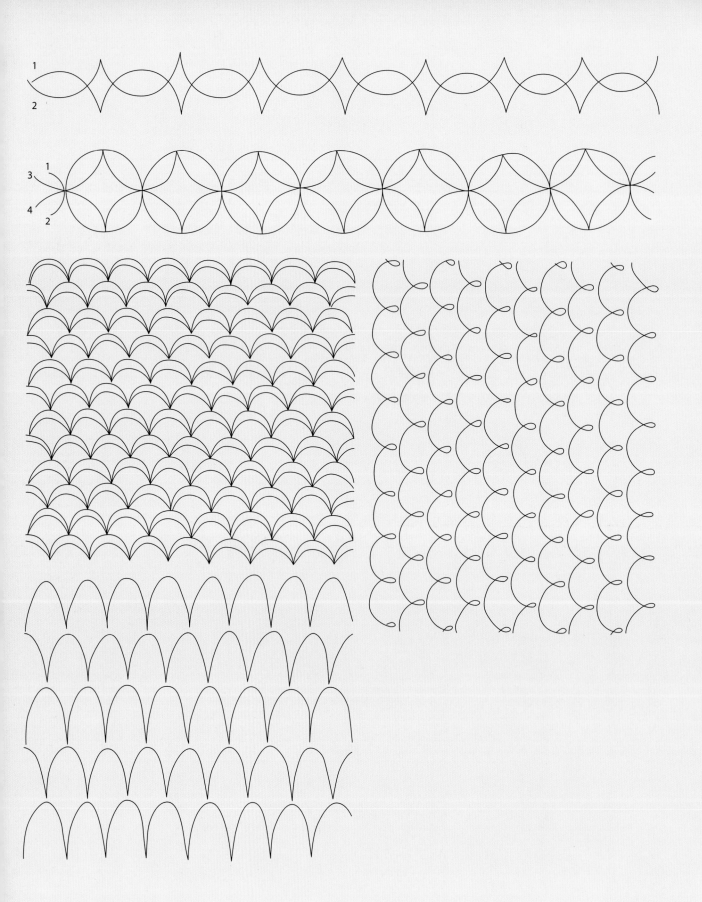

BRANCHING

In these designs a branch is stitched, and then a new branch leads off that branch, and so on. A branch can be as simple as a single teardrop or as complex as several spirals.

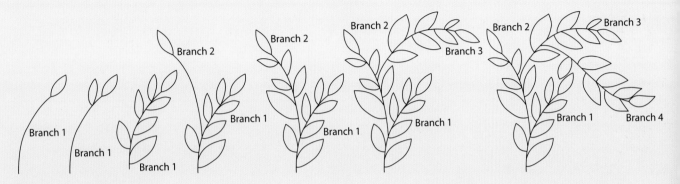

How to form branching designs

VINES AND FEATHERS

These designs feature decorative elements to either side of a central line. They are generally built from the bottom up. Changing what's on the vine or feather changes the look enormously. You can build vines and feathers with or without a spine stitched first.

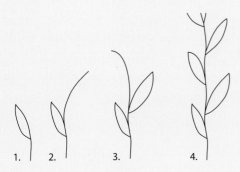

Simple vine stitched leaf by leaf

Simple feather stitched lobe by lobe, from bottom up

Simple vine stitched with spine first

Simple feather stitched with spine first

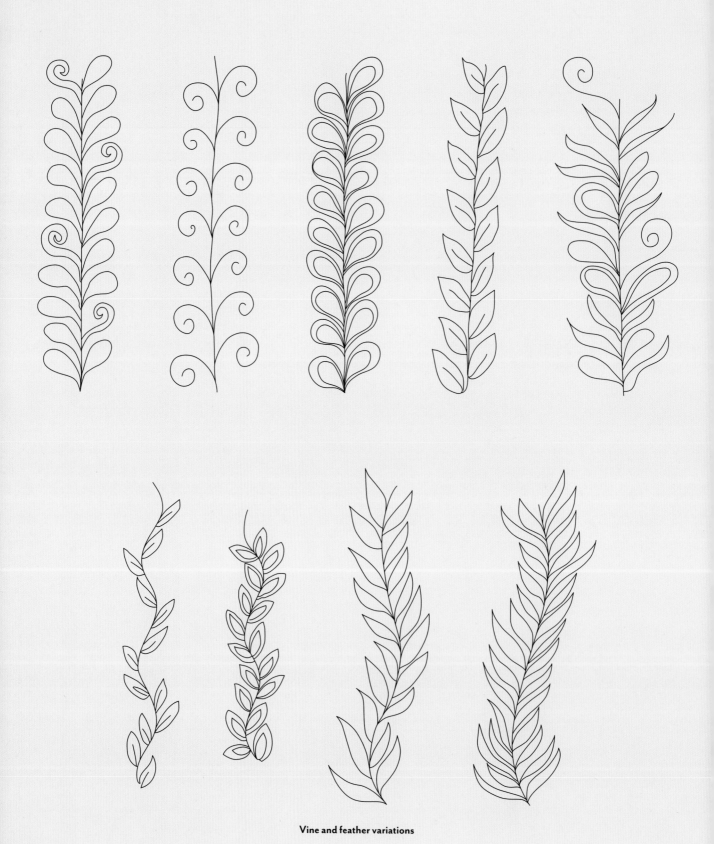

Vine and feather variations

SKETCHING AND WRITING

Drawing and writing in thread are fun challenges for the free-motion quilter. It takes some practice to get used to making these patterns with a continuous line. When writing, use cursive-style letters. Cross *T*'s as you form them. Dot *I*'s the same way, or come back and complete them separately. Connect words with a line at the bottom if needed.

When sketching, try taking two passes around the drawing to give definition to the sketch and to soften irregularities. Practice portraying the subject without getting bogged down in details.

Forming *T*'s and *I*'s, and connecting words

Some simple continuous-line sketches

Projects

The projects that follow are straightforward and not too fussy. Their simplicity invites you to get stitching. Adapt these directions as desired to suit your own style; change the stitching to the design you prefer, make the quilt the size you want, or come up with your own appliqué. Do whatever gets you excited about stitching. And have fun!

SMALL STITCHED PROJECTS

These projects are a great way to get a little quilting practice and
have something useful to show for it. They are perfect for using up
leftover pieces of batting, and they are ideal for first-time stitchers.

WIGGLE-BOTTOM CUSHION

Finished size: 14″ × 14″
Experience level: Brand new
Quilting design: Wavy lines

This cushion is quilted one strip at a time with simple wavy lines, making it a perfect beginner project. Foundation piecing the cushion top creates a strong base that can stand up to a lot of wear.

MATERIALS

Foundation fabric: 16″ × 16″

Batting: 20″ × 20″

Quilting backing (will not be seen): 20″ × 20″

Assorted scrap strips: 4″ to 24″ in length

Cushion backing fabric: ⅓ yard

1″ cushion foam: 13½″ × 13½″

Twill tape for ties: 1½ yard

MAKE IT

1. Lay a scrap strip face up on the foundation fabric, diagonally from corner to corner. Make sure the strip goes to the edges of the foundation fabric. Pin in place at the ends. *(See Figure A.)*

2. Lay another strip face down over the first, aligned with the right-hand raw edge of the first strip. Make sure this strip also goes to the edges of the foundation fabric. With the machine set for straight stitching, sew with a ¼″ seam allowance. *(See Figure B.)*

3. Flip the second strip over and press. *(See Figure C.)*

4. Lay a new strip face down so that a raw edge is aligned with the raw edge of the last strip you added. Stitch, flip, and press. *(See Figure D.)*

5. Repeat Step 4 until you have covered half of the foundation fabric.

6. Rotate the square, and repeat Steps 2–5 to cover the other half.

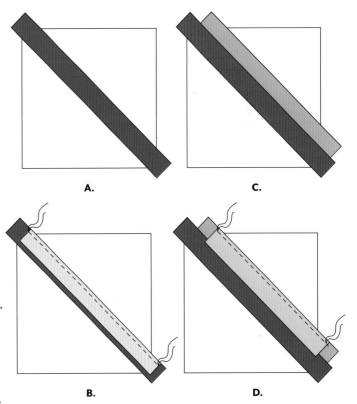

A.

C.

B.

D.

7. Turn the foundation piece right side down and trim the edges of the fabric strips down to the sides of the foundation square. *(See Figure E.)*

8. Layer the pieced square, the batting, and the quilting backing. Baste. See Layering and Basting Quilts and Projects (page 137).

9. With the machine set for free-motion quilting, quilt a wavy line in each strip. Cut the quilted piece to 15″ × 15″ square.

10. From the twill tape, cut 4 ties 12″ long. Knot an end of each tie.

11. Cut 2 pieces 10½″ × 15″ from the cushion backing fabric. On each piece, turn a 15″ edge down ¾″ and press; then turn down and press again, so the raw edge is encased in the fold. Topstitch.

12. Lay the cushion top face up on the work area. Place the unknotted ends of 2 ties 3½″ in from each corner along the back edge. Then, on top of the ties, layer the cushion backing pieces, right side down and raw edges aligned, so that they overlap in the middle, creating an envelope opening. *(See Figure F.)*

13. With the machine set for straight stitching, sew around the entire piece with a ⅜″ seam.

14. Turn project right side out and insert foam cushion.

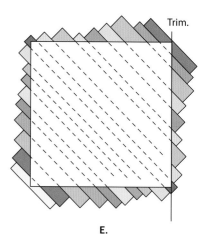

Trim.

E.

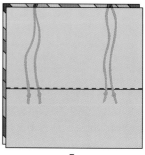

F.

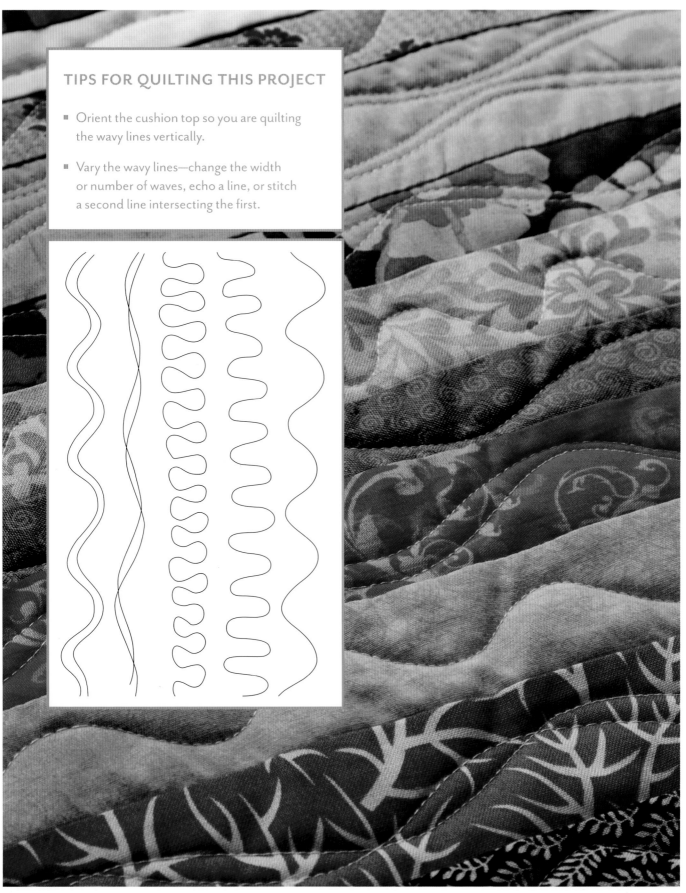

TIPS FOR QUILTING THIS PROJECT

- Orient the cushion top so you are quilting the wavy lines vertically.

- Vary the wavy lines—change the width or number of waves, echo a line, or stitch a second line intersecting the first.

REVERSE-STITCHED TABLE RUNNER

Finished size: 13″ × 39″
Experience level: Getting it
Quilting design: Determined by print fabric

Stitching along the lines of a print fabric, such as this one by Jane Sassaman, can create captivating designs on the reverse side.

MATERIALS

Print for quilting design / table runner backing: ½ yard*

Print fabric for front: 1 fat quarter

Contrast fabric for front: ½ yard

Batting: 3 pieces 16″ × 16″

Sashing: ¼ yard

Binding: ⅓ yard

Walking foot (recommended)

* Requires 42″ usable fabric width

CUTTING

1. Cut print fabric for quilting design / backing into 3 pieces 14″ × 14″.

2. Cut 2 pieces 16″ × 16″ from contrast fabric for front. Cut a piece 16″ × 16″ from print fabric for front.

3. From sashing fabric, cut 2 pieces 2″ × 13½″ and 2 pieces 3″ × 13½″.

MAKE IT

1. Layer each square of quilting design / backing fabric with batting squares and front fabrics. Baste. See Layering and Basting Quilts and Projects (page 137). With the machine set for free-motion quilting, quilt all 3 squares, following the lines of the quilting design fabric.

2. Cut quilted pieces down to 13″ × 13″.

3. With the machine set for straight stitching, join sashing and squares together using the Quilt-as-You-Go Method (page 112). Use a walking foot if you have it.

4. Bind the runner. See Binding a Finished Quilt (page 138).

Stitching along printed fabric and reverse side

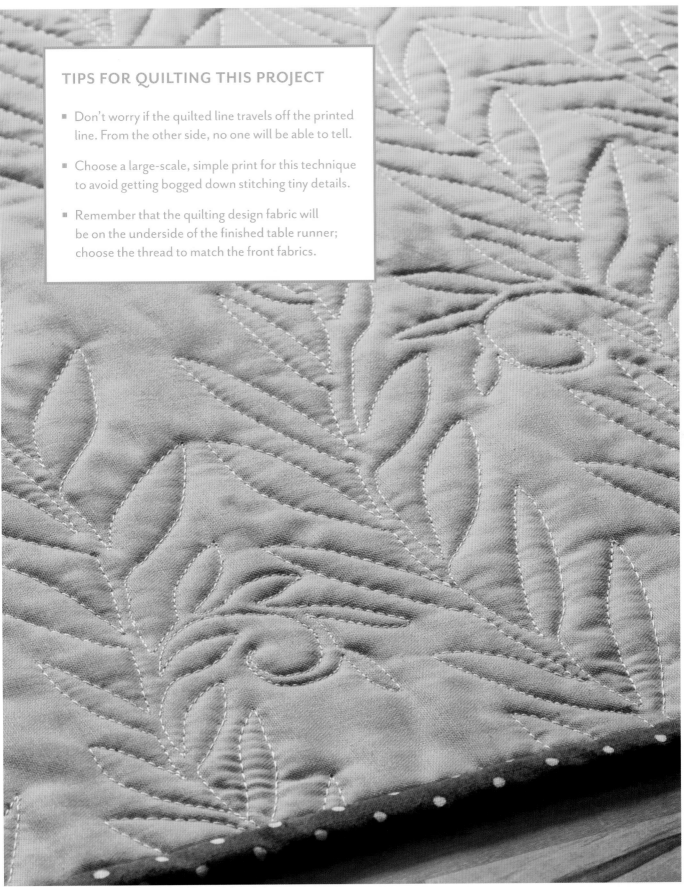

TIPS FOR QUILTING THIS PROJECT

- Don't worry if the quilted line travels off the printed line. From the other side, no one will be able to tell.

- Choose a large-scale, simple print for this technique to avoid getting bogged down stitching tiny details.

- Remember that the quilting design fabric will be on the underside of the finished table runner; choose the thread to match the front fabrics.

FISHBOWL PURSE

Finished size: 8″ wide × 6½″ high × 1½″ deep

Experience level: Brand new

Quilting design: Stretchy meandering

This lighthearted purse really gives me a thrill.
It's such a departure from the typical quilted bag!

MATERIALS

Blue fabric for fishbowl: 12″ × 24″

Batting: 16″ × 28″

Backing of quilted piece (will not be seen): 16″ × 28″

Bag lining: ¼ yard

Woven trim for strap: 1″ wide × 12″ long

Lightweight fusible web: 3″ × 6″

Fabric scrap for fish: 4″ × 7″

MAKE IT

1. Layer the fishbowl fabric, the batting, and the quilting backing. Baste. See Layering and Basting Quilts and Projects (page 137). With the machine set for free-motion quilting, quilt the entire piece.

2. Using the pattern (page 61), cut 2 bowl pieces from the quilted piece and a long strip 2″ × 22″. Do the same with the lining fabric.

3. Cut a piece of fusible web 3″ × 6″. Fuse to the fish fabric scrap. Trace 2 copies of the fish design (page 61) onto the paper side of the fusible web. Cut out. See Fusible Appliqué (page 135). Fuse a fish piece to the front of each fishbowl piece, being sure to keep the longer of the fishbowl edges to the top. Keep the appliqués clear of the ¼″ seam allowance you will need to sew the quilted pieces together.

4. With the machine set for a zigzag stitch, sew around the fish to secure them.

5. With the machine set for straight stitching, join the long strip to a fishbowl piece, right sides together, starting at a top corner and going around the bottom to the other top corner. Cut off any excess strip. Add the second fishbowl piece to the other side of the strip, making sure to align corners. Repeat with the lining pieces.

6. Turn the quilted piece right side out. Lay the ends of the strap against the outside edges of the bag, with the raw edges aligned. The body of the strap should point down and around the outside of the bag. Make sure the strap is not twisted. Baste to the bag body within the outer ¼″ of the top edge.

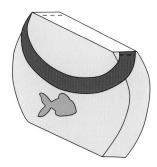

7. With the lining piece wrong side out, slip the quilted piece inside the lining piece so that the right sides are together. Make sure the body of the strap is below the raw edge. Pin the pieces in place. Sew around the top raw edge with a ¼″ seam allowance, leaving a 4″ space for turning along a straight edge. Turn the piece right side out and press the top edge, turning the open edge under ¼″.

8. Topstitch around the entire top edge to close the opening.

TIP FOR QUILTING THIS PROJECT

The quilting is a stretchy meandering pattern with lots of wiggles and occasional loose spirals to give the feel of water. Work with the short ends of the piece at the top and bottom, and stitch the design parallel to the long edge of the quilted piece.

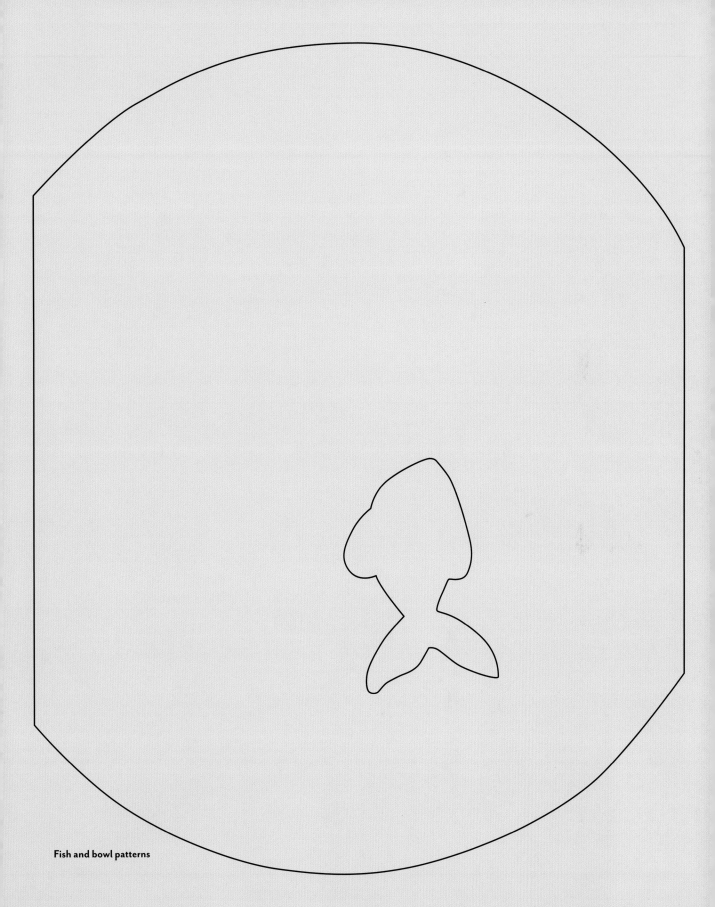

Fish and bowl patterns

BOTANICAL PLACE MATS

Finished size: Set of 4 place mats, 14″ × 19″ each
Experience level: Getting it
Quilting design: Vines and feathers

These place mats are the perfect way to practice vine and feather designs. Choosing leafy, organic patterns makes stitching variations look natural.

MATERIALS

Front: ¼ yard each of 6 different fabrics

Backing of quilted pieces* (will not be seen): 1 yard

Batting: 2 pieces 22″ × 34″

Place mat backing: 1 yard

* Requires 44″-wide fabric

MAKE IT

1. From each front fabric cut 2 strips 3¾″ × 30″.

2. With the machine set for straight stitching, piece strips together into 2 sets of 6 strips each. Press.

3. Cut backing for quilted pieces into 2 pieces 22″ × 34″.

4. Layer pieced sections with batting and quilting backing. Baste. See Layering and Basting Quilts and Projects (page 137).

5. With the machine set for free-motion quilting, quilt individual vines or feathers in each strip.

6. Cut 2 place mat pieces 14½″ × 19½″ from each quilted piece for a total of 4. Cut 4 equal-sized pieces of fabric for the place mat backing. Lay a backing piece on each place mat piece, right sides together.

7. With the machine set for straight stitching, sew around all sides, leaving a 5″ opening on a side for turning.

8. Clip excess fabric from corners and turn right side out. Press, turning the raw edges at the opening under ¼″. Use a ladder stitch (page 136) to close the side opening.

TIPS FOR QUILTING THIS PROJECT

- Start from the top of each strip and quilt the centerline down toward the bottom. Then travel back up that line to add the leaves or designs to the sides.

- Keep the design ¼″ in from the right and left edges of the quilted pieces to allow for the loss of the seam allowance when finishing the place mats.

LOOPY BUCKET

Finished size: 6″ wide × 7″ high × 6″ deep
Experience level: Brand new
Quilting design: Edge-to-edge loops

This simple bucket is so quick to finish, you'll find yourself making it again and again.

MATERIALS

Linen: 13″ × 21″

Batting: 16″ × 24″

Backing for quilted piece (will not be seen): 16″ × 24″

Lining fabric: 12″ × 20″

Assorted scraps: 1½″–3½″ wide × 6″ long

Temporary fabric marker

MAKE IT

1. Make a mark with a temporary fabric marker along the edge of the linen piece, halfway down each of the long sides, to identify the midline. Layer the linen, batting, and quilting backing, and baste. See Layering and Basting Quilts and Projects (page 137).

2. With the machine set for free-motion quilting, quilt lines of loops that run parallel to the short ends of the piece. The first lines you quilt should be ¾″ from the midline. The loops should extend away from the midline of the quilted piece, pointing toward the short sides in both directions. Place lines 1½″ apart.

3. Cut quilted piece down to 12″ × 20″, keeping the midline centered. Fold in half along the midline, right sides together, so the 12″ sides meet at the top. With the machine set for straight stitching, sew side seams with a ¼″ seam allowance, leaving the top open.

4. Mark a rectangle on each folded corner 3″ high × 3¼″ wide. Cut these corners out. *(See Figure A.)*

5. Reshape the piece to bring the cut-out edges of a corner together in a straight line. The sewn seam should be centered. Stitch the corner closed. *(See Figure B.)* Repeat on the other corner. Turn right side out.

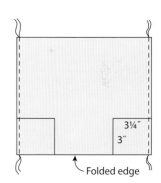

3¼″

3″

Folded edge

A.

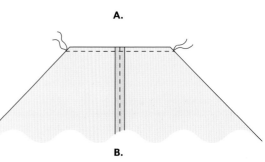

B.

6. Repeat Steps 3–5 with the lining fabric, but leave the completed lining piece wrong side out. Place the lining in the quilted bucket, wrong sides together.

7. Sew scraps together along their long sides to create a pieced strip 24″ long. Trim to 5″ × 23½″. Sew together the short ends of the scrappy strip, right sides together, to create a loop. Fold the loop in half lengthwise, wrong sides together, and press.

8. Nestle the folded scrappy loop inside the bucket lining with raw edges aligned at the top. Stitch around the entire top of the bucket, through all 3 layers. Flip the scrappy strip over the raw edge.

TIPS FOR QUILTING THIS PROJECT

- Try stitching alternating bigger and smaller loops. This approach allows for irregularity and is more forgiving than making every loop the same size.

- Use a piece of masking tape to help keep the lines level. See Creating Regularly Spaced Designs (page 21).

GIFT BAGS

Finished sizes:

    Small bag, 5″ × 7½″

    Medium bag, 7″ × 9½″

    Large bag, 8½″ × 11¾″

Experience level: Brand new

Quilting design: Determined by print fabric

Using prints to guide stitching is a great way to get a feel for free-motion quilting.

MATERIALS

	Small bag	Medium bag	Large bag
Fabric for bag	8″ × 18″	10″ × 22″	12″ × 27″
Batting	12″ × 22″	14″ × 26″	16″ × 31″
Back of quilted piece*	12″ × 22″	14″ × 26″	16″ × 31″
Lining (cut 2)	7″ × 10½″	9″ × 12½″	11″ × 15″
1″ Ribbon (cut 2)	12″	14″	17″

* Will not be seen

MAKE IT

1. Layer the bag fabric, the batting, and the quilting backing. Baste. See Layering and Basting Quilts and Projects (page 137). With the machine set for free-motion quilting, quilt the piece following the printed design.

2. Cut 2 bag pieces from the quilted piece as follows:

    Small bag: Cut 2 pieces 7″ × 8½″.

    Medium bag: Cut 2 pieces 9″ × 10½″.

    Large bag: Cut 2 pieces 11″ × 13″.

3. Place ribbon handles on a short edge of each quilted piece. Align raw edges at the top and tack in place with a pin or glue. Measure the distance from the side edge of the quilted piece to the ribbon edge as follows:

    Small bag: 1¾″

    Medium bag: 2¼″

    Large bag: 2¾″

4. On the wrong side of each lining piece, mark a horizontal line 1″ from the top (a short edge). Lay a lining piece over each quilted piece, right sides together, with top raw edges aligned. The ribbons will be between the 2 pieces. Pin in place. With the machine set for straight stitching, sew along marked lines. Open and press seam.

5. Lay bag pieces right sides together, matching seams. Sew around all 4 sides, leaving a 5″ opening in the lining bottom for turning.

6. Box corners of quilted pieces at the following widths. See Boxing Corners (page 136). It is not necessary to box the lining pieces.

> **Small bag:** 1½″
> **Medium bag:** 1½″
> **Large bag:** 2″

7. Turn right side out and stitch the hole in the lining closed. Press top edge and corners to give the bag definition.

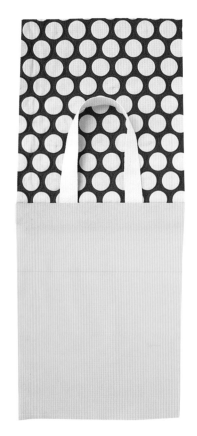

TIP FOR QUILTING THIS PROJECT

Look for motifs you can stitch around without
having to precisely follow tiny lines. Prints with
open space around regularly placed wavy lines,
dots, or scallops are ideal.

PEBBLE PILLOW

Finished size: 16½″ × 16½″
Experience level: Getting it
Quilting design: Pebbles

Pebbles are such a captivating design that they need little fanfare. Stitching individual rows in different colors gives a simple, strong impact.

MATERIALS

Fabric for pillow front: 17″ × 17″

Batting: 19″ × 19″

Back of quilted piece (will not be seen): 19″ × 19″

Fabric for pillow back: ½ yard

Binding: ¼ yard

Temporary fabric pencil or marker

16″ pillow form

Walking foot (recommended)

MAKE IT

1. Make 4 marks on each edge of the pillow front, measuring them 2½″ and 6½″ away from each corner. Mark diagonal lines connecting the points with a ruler and a temporary fabric marker.

2. Layer the pillow front with the batting and the quilting backing. Baste. See Layering and Basting Quilts and Projects (page 137).

3. With the machine set for straight stitching, sew along the marked lines. Use a walking foot if you have it. Remove any marked lines that are visible after you have stitched over them.

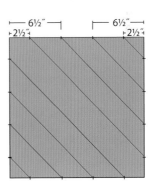

4. With the machine set for free-motion quilting, quilt the pillow top. Switch thread colors between columns.

5. Trim the quilted piece to 16½″ × 16½″ square.

6. From the pillow backing fabric, cut 2 pieces 11″ × 16½″.

7. On each backing piece, fold down ½″ along a long side and press; then fold once more and press again, so the raw edge is contained within the fold. With the machine set for straight stitching, topstitch.

8. Lay the quilted piece face down, and then place the pillow backing pieces on it, right side up. Align the raw edges. The finished edges of the backing pieces will overlap in the center, creating an envelope opening.

9. Pin pillow backing pieces in place. With the machine set for straight stitching, sew around the pillow with a scant ¼″ seam to secure pillow front and backing pieces together.

10. Bind (page 138) and insert pillow form.

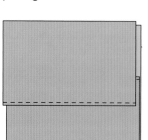

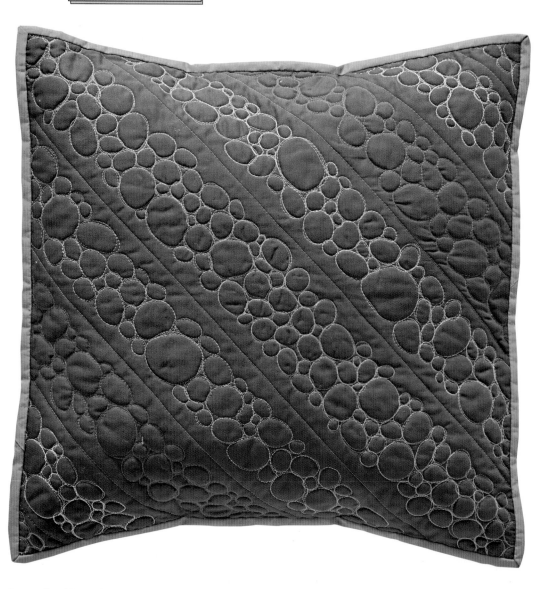

TIPS FOR QUILTING THIS PROJECT

- When pebbles are very small they take a long time to stitch. Vary the size of the pebbles, making sure to include some larger ones as you start off.

- Stitching around each pebble twice before moving on to the next will give definition and depth to the pattern.

- Leave some space between the pebbles and the straight lines.

LITTLE BOWLS

Approximate finished sizes: 5″ diameter × 1¼″ high to 8″ diameter × 1¼″ high
Experience level: Brand new
Quilting design: Spirals

Any circular quilted piece can be shaped into a reversible bowl in no time. These are fat quarter–friendly and perfect for basting pins, bobbins, and buttons. As long as you don't get too large or too small, any circle size will do. Trace around a plate or bowl for an easy circle template.

MATERIALS

Circular object for tracing: 7½″–10½″ diameter

Inner fabric: Large enough for the circle you are tracing, between 8″ × 8″ and 11″ × 11″

Outer fabric: 2″ larger than inner fabric square, between 10″ × 10″ and 13″ × 13″

Batting: 2″ larger than inner fabric square, between 10″ × 10″ and 13″ × 13″

Binding fabric: ⅛ yard

Fabric marker

MAKE IT

1. Trace a circle onto the inner fabric with a fabric marker. Place on top of the batting and backing, and baste together. See Layering and Basting Quilts and Projects (page 137).

2. Find the center of the circle and mark with a pin. With the machine set for free-motion quilting, quilt a spiral starting from the center spot, until you have filled the marked circle. Cut out the circle on the marked line.

3. With the machine set for straight stitching, stitch around the circle once using a long basting stitch. Start with long thread tails and leave the thread tails long when you cut at the end. Starting just inward from the first stitching line, stitch around again, leaving thread tails long as before. Make sure to stitch both lines less than ¼″ from the edge. Do not let the basting lines overlap and do not backstitch or stitch over the starting stitches when you come back to the starting point.

4. Carefully pull the basting threads to gather the circle evenly into a bowl shape. When the desired shape is reached, tie the threads together to keep them from loosening while you attach the binding.

5. Bind the bowl. See Binding a Finished Quilt (page 138). Attach the binding to the inside of the bowl, and flip it to the outside for finishing.

TIPS FOR STITCHING THIS PROJECT

- If the base of your darning foot is round, you can use its outer edge as a guide to keep the spiral even as you work outward.

- If keeping the spiral design even seems difficult, stitch a different pattern instead.

ZIGZAG POTHOLDERS

Finished size: Set of 2 potholders, 9″ × 9″ each
Experience level: Brand new
Quilting design: Edge-to-edge zigzags

Double-thickness potholders are a perfect reason to practice free-motion quilting.

MATERIALS

Potholder fabric: 10½″ × 10½″ each of 4 different fabrics

Batting: 4 pieces each 12½″ × 12½″ (*optional*—use Insul-Fleece by C&T Publishing instead of batting for insulated layer)

Quilting backing (will not be seen): ¾ yard

Ribbon for hanging loops: 8″

Binding fabric: ¼ yard

MAKE IT

1. Stack all 4 potholder fabrics on top of each other, with edges aligned. Use a rotary cutter and ruler to make an angled cut from top to bottom.

2. Rearrange the pieces into matched pairs of mixed fabrics (A with B, B with A, C with D, D with C). With the machine set for straight stitching, join along the cut edge. Press.

3. Stack all 4 squares on top of each other again, with edges aligned and all the angled seams in the same orientation. Make another angled cut across the first seam.

4. Rearrange the pieces to make 4 squares, each of which contains all the initial fabrics. Join along the cut edge. Press.

5. Cut 4 quilting backing fabric pieces, each 12½″ × 12½″.

6. Layer each pieced square with batting or Insul-Fleece and quilting backing. Baste. See Layering and Basting Quilts and Projects (page 137).

7. With the machine set for free-motion quilting, quilt each square individually. Cut quilted squares to 9″ × 9″.

8. Layer 2 squares, backs together. Add a small loop of ribbon in a corner of each pair, with raw edges extending beyond the raw edge of the potholder, and the ribbon fold pointing toward the middle of the square. Stitch around the edges with a scant ¼″ seam. Cut off excess ribbon.

9. Bind potholders. See Binding a Finished Quilt (page 138).

TIPS FOR QUILTING THIS PROJECT

- Zigzags are fresh and simple. Don't worry too much about making them perfect; they will all blend together into an overall pattern when you step back.

- Orient the zigzag lines to run parallel to one of the angled seams in each square.

- Avoid pausing too long at the corners or you may see little balls of thread appear there from the extra stitches that happen during the pause.

WOOD GRAIN ZIPPER BAG

Finished size: 8½″ wide × 7″ high × 1½″ deep

Experience level: Brand new

Quilting design: Stretchy meandering

The delightful texture on this bag is a simple pattern for a beginner to stitch. It makes a great understated gift for the people in your life who are hard to sew for.

MATERIALS

Fabric for outer bag: 8½″ × 20″

Batting: 11″ × 23″

Quilting backing fabric (will not be seen): 11″ × 23″

Lining fabric: ¼ yard

9″ zipper

Scrap of outer fabric for zipper ends: 2″ × 4″

Zipper foot

MAKE IT

1. Layer the outer bag fabric, batting, and quilting backing. Baste. See Layering and Basting Quilts and Projects (page 137).

2. With the machine set for free-motion quilting, quilt the entire piece. Cut 2 pieces 7½″ × 9″ from the quilted piece. Cut 2 identically sized pieces from the lining fabric.

3. Unzip the zipper a few inches. Cut off the metal ends so that the zipper measures 8½″ long.

4. Fold the 2″ × 4″ scrap of outer fabric in half lengthwise, wrong sides together. Press. Open up and fold each raw edge in toward the pressed midline. Press again. Cut folded piece in half to create 2 double-folded pieces ½″ × 2″.

5. With the machine set for straight stitching, sew a folded piece around each end of the zipper. Trim the edges even with the zipper edge.

Trim.

6. Layer a quilted piece on top of the zipper with the right side of the zipper facing the right side of the quilted piece. Layer a lining piece beneath the zipper with the right side of the lining piece facing the wrong side of the zipper. Align the raw edges. Make sure the zipper is centered. Stitch this edge using a zipper foot.

7. Press the quilted piece away from the zipper. Topstitch the edge of the quilted piece, stitching only through the seam allowance of the lining. Keep the main body of the lining out of the seam.

8. Repeat Steps 6 and 7 on the other side of the zipper with the remaining quilted and lining pieces.

9. Open the zipper halfway. Lay the quilted pieces right sides together and the lining pieces right sides together with raw edges aligned. Nudge the bulk of the zipper toward the quilted pieces. Pin in place. Stitch around the entire bag and lining with a ¼″ seam allowance, leaving a 5″ hole for turning at the bottom of the lining.

10. Box the corners of the bag at a 1″ width. See Boxing Corners (page 136). It is not necessary to box the lining corners. Turn the bag right side out and stitch the lining closed.

TIPS FOR STITCHING THIS PROJECT

- Stitch the wood grain design parallel with the short edges of the piece.

- The organic nature of this design is great for beginners. Wobbles and inconsistencies fit right in! Start with a somewhat bumpy line going from top to bottom. Stitch another line to the side of that one. Let the line respond to the first line, exaggerating some of its bumps, and drawing nearer to and farther from it in places. Stitch another line next to that. Exaggerate some bumps even more, and insert a loose, wobbly spiral for a knot if there is a good place for it. Add more lines that flow toward, away from, or around the spiral. Continue with more bumpy lines and occasional points or knots until the piece is filled.

QUILTED MESSENGER BAG

Finished size: 10¾″ wide × 11¾″ high × 3″ deep
Experience level: Getting it
Quilting design: Paisley

I've kept these instructions as simple as possible so you can focus on the quilting. Add a closure or pockets if you want, but this is an opportunity to experiment with any quilting pattern you'd like to try.

MATERIALS

Fabric for bag: ½ yard

Backing for quilted pieces (will not be seen): 1 yard

Batting: 2 pieces 16″ × 19″ and 1 piece 16″ × 17″

Bag lining: ½ yard

1½″-wide woven strap: 45″

Fabric for appliqué: 5″ × 6″ each of 5 different fabrics

Lightweight fusible web: 5 pieces 4½″ × 5½″

CUTTING

1. From bag fabric, cut 1 piece 13″ × 14″ for the flap and 2 pieces 13″ × 16″ for the body.

2. From lining fabric, cut 1 piece 12″ × 13″ for the flap and 2 pieces 12″ × 15″ for the body.

MAKE IT

1. Fuse fusible web to the back side of appliqué fabrics. Using the pattern (at right), trace and cut 4 drop shapes, 2 from each side of the pattern, so that you have 2 right-leaning drops and 2 left-leaning drops in each color. See Fusible Appliqué (page 135).

2. Arrange appliqué pieces as desired on the bag flap piece. The flap fabric should be oriented with the longer edges at the sides. Keep all appliqué pieces in at least 1″ from the edge to account for trimming and seam allowances. You may not need all the appliqué pieces. Fuse the appliqué pieces to the flap fabric according to package directions. With the machine set for a zigzag stitch, sew around each appliqué piece.

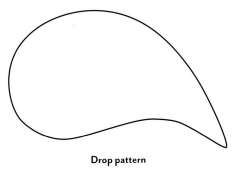

Drop pattern

3. From the backing for quilted pieces, cut 1 piece 16″ × 17″ for the flap and 2 pieces 16″ × 19″ for the body. Layer the bag flap and bag body pieces with batting and backing. Baste. See Layering and Basting Quilts and Projects (page 137).

4. With the machine set for free-motion quilting, quilt each section. Cut the bag flap to 12″ × 13″. Cut the bag body pieces to 12″ × 15″.

5. Lay the bag flap piece and bag flap lining right sides together. With the machine set for straight stitching, sew around the sides and bottom with

a ¼″ seam allowance, leaving the top open. Clip excess material from corners. Turn right side out, press, and topstitch around the sides and bottom.

6. Lay the body pieces of the bag right sides together, and sew together along the sides and bottom. Box the corners at 3″ wide. See Boxing Corners (page 136). Repeat with the bag lining pieces.

7. Turn the bag body right side out. Lay the strap ends at the sides of the bag body so the side seam is aligned in the center of the strap. Make sure the strap is not twisted. Align raw edges and use glue or a basting stitch to baste the straps to the bag body within the top ¼″ seam allowance.

8. Place the bag flap piece against the bag body back, right sides together, with raw edges aligned. Make sure the flap is centered. Use glue or a basting stitch to baste the flap to the bag body within the top ¼″ seam allowance.

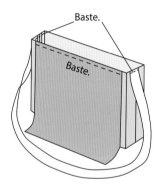

9. Set the entire bag body, flap, and strap inside the bag lining piece. The right sides should be together and the strap and flap should all be between the bag and lining, below the top edge.

10. Stitch around the top edge of the bag, leaving a 5″ hole in the front edge for turning.

11. Turn the bag right side out. Press edges, turning the open edges under ¼″. Topstitch around the entire bag top, closing the opening as you go.

TIPS FOR QUILTING THIS PROJECT

- Start by quilting the bag body pieces first so you've had some practice with the design by the time you quilt the front flap piece.

- When quilting the flap piece, start by tracing around the appliqué pieces. Then extend paisley shapes from the appliqué area so they radiate outward. When you reach the outside edge, restart from the appliqué section, to let the design continue to radiate outward.

GOOD ADVICE WALLHANGING

Finished size: 8″ × 9½″
Experience level: Comfortable
Quilting design: Pebbles, words

This saying gets me stitching when I'm worried about making mistakes. Do you have some good advice to stitch up?

MATERIALS

Background fabric: 10″ × 15″

Fabric scraps: 5 pieces 1¾″ wide, up to 4″ long

Batting: 12″ × 14″

Backing: 12″ × 14″

Binding: 2¼″ × width of fabric

Fabric for hanging pockets: 2 pieces 3½″ × 3½″

Dowel for hanging: 7″

CUTTING

1. From background fabric, cut 5 strips 1¾″ × 10″ and 2 strips 3″ × 10″. Cut each 1¾″ strip in half, into 2 pieces 1¾″ × 5″.

2. Cut the 1¾″-wide scraps to the following lengths: 3½″, 2½″, 4″, 3″, and 4″.

MAKE IT

1. Sew a 1¾″ × 5″ background strip to each short end of each fabric scrap. Arrange pieced strips in the order given in Step 2 of Cutting and align strips as desired. With the machine set for straight stitching, sew the strips together. Trim section to 9″ wide. Add a 3″ background strip to the top and bottom of the strip set. Trim edges even. Press.

2. Layer and baste. See Layering and Basting Quilts and Projects (page 137).

3. With the machine set for free-motion quilting, quilt the piece with words in the fabric scraps and a design in the background. Trim quilted piece to 8″ × 9½″.

4. Press hanging pockets in half diagonally, wrong sides together. Lay these on the back side of the quilted piece, in the top corners, with raw corner edges aligned. Baste in place with glue or stitching along the edge within the outer ¼″.

5. Bind. See Binding a Finished Quilt (page 138).

- Start by practicing the words on a practice pad. Make sure they will fit in the space you have. Then quilt the words on the wallhanging.

- For the pebbles, begin stitching around the perimeter of the center section. Continue working around the piece from the middle outward until you have quilted the entire area.

- Add an asterisk in the middle of an occasional large pebble.

6. Insert the dowel into the hanging pockets. Hang the finished piece by resting the dowel over 2 level nails or hooks.

SIMPLE QUILTS

When you're ready to put something a little larger under the

machine, try one of these simple lap or baby-sized quilts.

The piecing goes fast, so you can spend your time quilting.

STRIP SAMPLER

Finished size: 40″ × 54″
Experience level: Brand new
Quilting design: Various

Make this quilt out of whatever fabrics you have around, cutting strips straight across the fabric width. Stitch a different pattern in each strip for a fast and fun sampler quilt.

MATERIALS

4 large strips of fabric, 6″ to 8½″ × width of fabric

5 medium strips of fabric, 3″ to 4½″ × width of fabric

8 small strips of fabric, 1½″ to 2½″ × width of fabric

Backing: 2¾ yards pieced to 46″ × 60″

Batting: 46″ × 60″

Binding: ½ yard

MAKE IT

1. Vary the sizes of the strips so the quilt is approximately 54″ long. Arrange the strips from top to bottom as follows:

Medium, Small, Large, Small,
Medium, Small, Large, Small,
Medium, Small, Large, Small,
Medium, Small, Large, Small,
Medium

2. With the machine set for straight stitching, sew strips together in pairs, Strip 1 to Strip 2, Strip 3 to Strip 4, and so on. Sew pairs of strips together into 4-strip sections. Sew sections together until the quilt top is complete. Press.

3. Square up the sides so the quilt is 40″ wide. Layer quilt top, batting, and backing. Baste. See Layering and Basting Quilts and Projects (page 137).

4. With the machine set for free-motion quilting, quilt each strip individually, using a different pattern in each strip.

5. Bind. See Binding a Finished Quilt (page 138).

TIPS FOR QUILTING THIS PROJECT

- Large strips are great for practicing allover designs such as meandering and branching patterns.

- Medium strips are ideal for more intricate designs, such as pebbles, vines, or feathers.

- Small strips are good for spirals, zigzags, and lines of loops.

BIG SQUARE

Finished size: 43″ × 43″
Experience level: Getting it
Quilting design: Meandering

This is a quick quilt top for jumping in to practice an allover design such as meandering. It's the perfect way to feature a beloved large-scale print, such as this Joel Dewberry floral.

MATERIALS

Center print: 1 fat quarter

Inner border: ⅛ yard

Outer border: 1⅛ yards

Batting: 49″ × 49″

Backing: 3 yards pieced to 49″ × 49″

Binding: ⅜ yard

CUTTING

1. From center print, cut an 18″ × 18″ square.

2. From inner border fabric, cut 2 strips 1½″ × width of fabric. From these strips, cut 2 pieces 18″ each and 2 pieces 20″ each.

3. From outer border fabric, cut 3 strips 12″ × width of fabric. From 1 strip, cut 2 pieces 20″ each. Cut the 2 remaining strips to 43″. If the strips are shorter than 43″, piece additional fabric to each strip to make them long enough.

MAKE IT

1. With the machine set for straight stitching, sew an 18″ inner border strip to the top and bottom of the center strip. Press. Sew remaining inner border strips to the sides. Press.

2. Sew a 20″ outer border strip to the top and bottom of the piece. Press. Sew remaining outer border strips to the sides. Press.

3. Layer quilt top, batting, and backing. Baste. See Layering and Basting Quilts and Projects (page 137).

4. With the machine set for free-motion quilting, quilt the center square and the outer border. Leave the inner border unquilted.

5. Bind. See Binding a Finished Quilt (page 138).

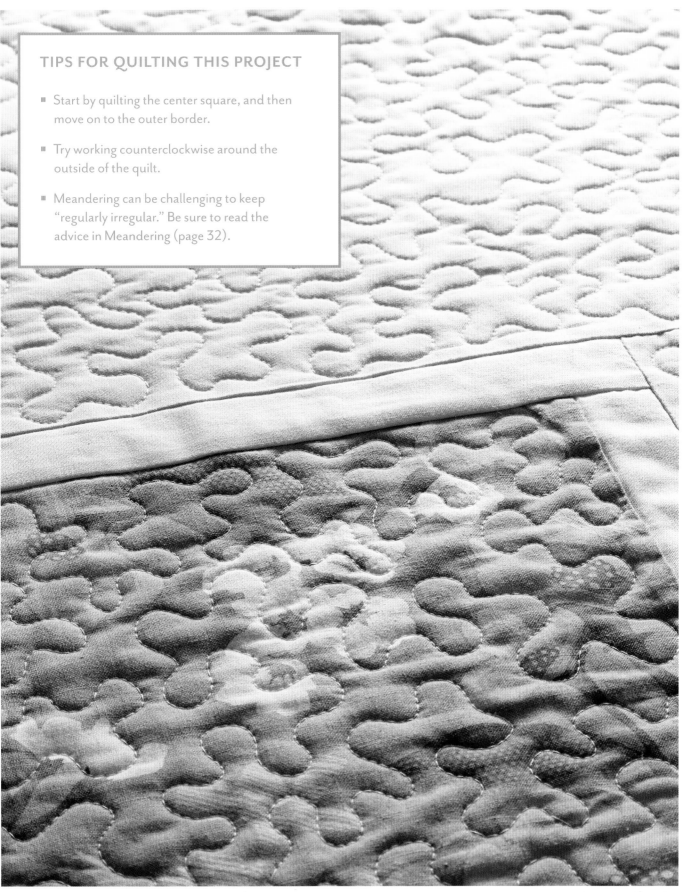

TIPS FOR QUILTING THIS PROJECT

- Start by quilting the center square, and then move on to the outer border.

- Try working counterclockwise around the outside of the quilt.

- Meandering can be challenging to keep "regularly irregular." Be sure to read the advice in Meandering (page 32).

FIREWORKS

Finished size: 40″ × 54″
Experience level: Getting it
Quilting design: Spirals, thread sketching

Light thread against a dark background makes these fireworks sparkle!

MATERIALS

Fabric for quilt top: 1⅝ yards

Batting: 46″ × 60″

Backing: 2¾ yards pieced to 46″ × 60″

Binding: ½ yard

Fabric for circles: 8″ × 11″ each of
5 different fabrics

Lightweight fusible web: 5 pieces 7″ × 10″

CUTTING

Cut fabric for quilt top to 40″ × 54″.

MAKE IT

1. Fuse a piece of fusible web to each piece of appliqué fabric. Trace and cut out 4 circles from each fabric, for a total of 6 large, 6 medium, and 8 small circles. (Patterns are at right.) See Fusible Appliqué (page 135).

2. Press quilt top. Arrange the circles and fuse to the quilt top following package directions.

3. Layer quilt top, batting, and backing. Baste. See Layering and Basting Quilts and Projects (page 137).

4. With the machine set for free-motion quilting, quilt around the edge of each circle, and then quilt a starburst design radiating from each appliqué. Use light-colored thread for this step.

5. Using a thread that blends with the quilt top, quilt the remainder of the top.

6. Bind. See Binding a Finished Quilt (page 138).

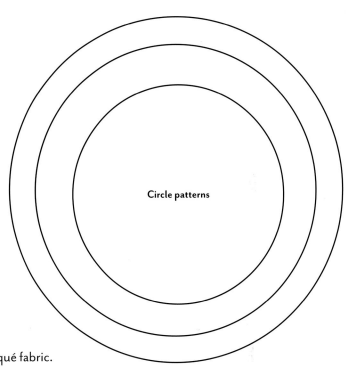

Circle patterns

QUILT-AS-YOU-GO QUILT

Finished size: 60" × 60"
Experience level: Brand new
Quilting design: Various

What if you quilted first and assembled the quilt afterward? This "quilt-as-you-go" method allows you to maneuver smaller portions of the quilt at once. It's a great way to do short stints of quilting and still end up with a big, beautiful quilt.

MATERIALS

Fabric for squares: ⅞ yard each of 9 different colors

Sashing: 2⅛ yards

Binding: ⅞ yard

Batting: 9 pieces 15" × 42"

Fabric marker

Walking foot (recommended for Quilt-as-You-Go Method, page 112)

CUTTING

1. From each of the main fabrics, cut a strip 15" and a strip 13" across the width of fabric.

2. Cut the 13" strips to 13" × 39".

3. From the sashing fabric, cut 14 strips 2" across the width of fabric and 14 strips 3" across the width of fabric.

4. From the 2" strips, set aside 4 to remain uncut. From the remaining strips, cut 4 pieces 2" × 21" and 20 pieces 2" × 12½".

5. Cut the 3" strips as described above for the 2" strips.

MAKE IT

1. On each 13″ × 39″ strip of main fabric, mark a line 13″ in from each short end, to make 3 sections for quilting on each strip. Layer each strip with batting and a 15″ strip. Baste. See Layering and Basting Quilts and Projects (page 137).

TIP

If you are not using yardage, make individual quilt sandwiches of a 13″ × 13″ top piece with 15″ × 15″ pieces of batting and backing.

----

2. With the machine set for free-motion quilting, quilt each section individually with any desired design.

3. From the quilted strips, cut quilted squares 12″ × 12″. You will have a total of 27 quilted squares. Only 25 are needed for the quilt, so eliminate your 2 least favorites! Arrange squares as desired into 5 rows of 5 squares each.

4. With the machine set for straight stitching, join a short end of a 21″ sashing strip to a short end of each width-of-fabric strip, trimming as needed to give 4 strips 60½″ long in both the 2″ and the 3″ widths.

5. Use the Quilt-as-You-Go Method (at right) to join quilted squares together. First create horizontal rows of 5 squares each, and then join those rows together.

6. Bind quilt with a wide ½″ binding. (Follow the method in Binding a Finished Quilt, page 138, but use strips 3¾″ wide and stitch ½″ from the raw edge. At the corners, stop stitching ½″ from the edge before folding the corner and proceeding as usual.)

QUILT-AS-YOU-GO METHOD

This method uses a ½″ seam allowance to create a 1″ sashing between sections. If your machine does not have a ½″ seam marking, use a piece of tape or a sticky note placed on the machine bed ½″ from the needle to serve as a seam guide. Try this technique on practice pieces first to ensure the seam allowance is accurate and that you are stitching through both top and bottom sashing strips in the final step. When joining larger sections, make sure the edges you are joining are very straight. Trim away bits of sashing and out-of-line edges as needed.

MATERIALS

Quilted pieces to join

Front sashing strip: 3″ × ½″ longer than the edge to be joined

Back sashing strip: 2″ × ½″ longer than the edge to be joined

Temporary fabric glue (gluestick or white glue will work fine)

Walking foot (recommended)

JOIN THE QUILTED PIECES

1. Press the 3″ front strip in half lengthwise, wrong sides together. Lay this on top of the first quilted piece along the edge to be joined. Lay the 2″ back strip beneath the quilted piece, right side to the quilted piece, along the edge to be joined. Align raw edges. Stitch all 3 layers with a ½″ seam allowance. Trim away the strips that extend beyond the edges of the quilted piece. *(See Figure A.)*

2. Press the 2″ back sashing strip away from the quilted piece. *(See Figure B.)* Lay the first quilted piece on top of the second quilted piece, backs together and raw edges aligned. Stitch the back sashing piece to the second quilted piece using a ½″ seam allowance.

3. Lay the joined pieces flat, back sides up. Press the back sashing. Turn the piece over. The raw edges of the 2 quilted squares should just meet. If there is any overlap, trim away only enough to allow the pieces to lie flat. Press the front sashing strip over the joined edges. Use a small amount of glue to tack the folded edge of the front sashing strip to the seam allowance of the second quilted piece. Make sure the folded edge reaches the line of stitching. Allow glue to dry. *(See Figure C.)*

4. Topstitch along both edges of the top sashing strips. *(See Figure D.)*

A. Sew sashing strips to front and back of block. Trim.

B. Press 2″ back sashing strip away from block.

C. Use glue to tack down folded edge.

D. Topstitch.

SECOND STAR TO THE RIGHT

Finished size: 40″ × 51″

Experience level: Getting it

Quilting design: Kissing stars

The empty space of this quilt allows the energetic stitching pattern to shine forth! Don't worry about matching up seams on the free-pieced stars. Let them be a little wonky.

MATERIALS

Background fabric: 2⅛ yards

Star fabric: ⅛ yard each of 2 different colors

Batting: 46″ × 57″

Backing: 2⅞ yards pieced to 46″ × 57″

Binding: ½ yard

CUTTING

1. From background fabric, cut strips the following sizes across the width of the fabric: 16″, 14½″, 9½″, and 3″.

2. From the 16″ strip, cut 1 square 16″ × 16″ and 1 square 11″ × 11″.

3. From the 14½″ strip, cut 1 piece 10″ × 14½″ and 1 piece 16½″ × 14½″.

4. From the 9½″ strip, cut 1 piece 5″ × 9½″ and 1 piece 26½″ × 9½″.

5. Cut 1 piece 25½″ × 40″ from the remaining background fabric.

6. Cut 6 rectangles 4″ × 6½″ from each of the star fabrics.

MAKE IT

1. On the 2 cut background fabric squares, make marks on the left and right edges. The marks on the 16″ square should be 3″ from the top and bottom corners. The marks on the 11″ square should be 2″ from the top and bottom corners.

2. Using a rotary cutter and ruler, cut 2 diagonal lines across each square, connecting the marked points. Then make a final vertical cut through the center of the square.

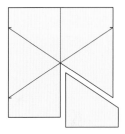

3. Construct star points: Remove a piece of a cut square. Lay a rectangle of star fabric over it, right sides together, as shown. With the machine set for straight stitching, sew an angled line from 1 cut edge to the other. Flip sewn piece over and press.

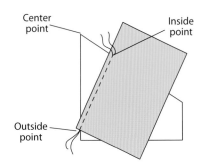

Center point

Inside point

Outside point

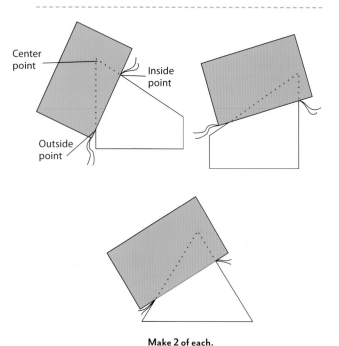

Make 2 of each.

4. Flip unit to the back side and trim even with the sides of the pointed background piece.

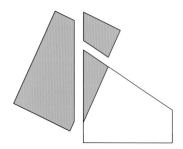

5. Cut away the excess fabric beneath the star fabric, leaving a ¼″ seam allowance. Repeat Steps 3–5 with all sections of each square.

6. Piece the sections together 3 at a time to form half-blocks. Piece the half-blocks together to make complete star blocks. Trim the larger block to 14½″ × 14½″ square. Trim the smaller block to 9½″ × 9½″ square.

7. Assemble quilt according to the diagram.

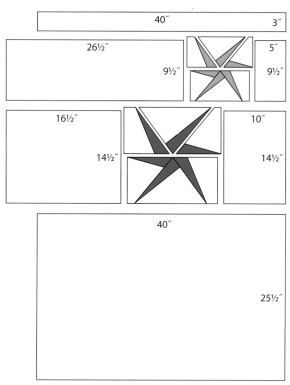

8. Layer the quilt top, batting, and backing. Baste. See Layering and Basting Quilts and Projects (page 137).

9. With the machine set for free-motion quilting, quilt. Bind. See Binding a Finished Quilt (page 138).

TIPS FOR QUILTING THIS PROJECT

- The variations in the pieced stars set the stage for variations in the star quilting.

- When the quilting approaches the pieced stars, quilt a line close around the entire perimeter of each star, but leave the stars themselves unquilted, allowing them to pop forward.

First Steps to Free-Motion Quilting

LEAVES

Finished size: 40″ × 54″

Experience level: Getting it

Quilting design: Branches, thread sketching

Sketchy quilting over appliqué has a wonderfully natural feel.

MATERIALS

Fabric for quilt top: 1⅝ yards

Batting: 46″ × 60″

Quilt backing: 2¾ yards pieced to 46″ × 60″

Binding: ½ yard

Fabric for leaves: 6″ × 9″ each of 5 fabrics

Lightweight fusible web: 5 pieces 5″ × 8″

CUTTING

Cut fabric for quilt top to 40″ × 54″.

MAKE IT

1. Fuse web to appliqué fabric. Trace and cut 3 leaves from each piece of appliqué fabric. (The pattern is at right.) See Fusible Appliqué (page 135).

2. Press quilt top. Arrange the leaves on the quilt top. Pin in place, and then fuse, following the manufacturer's directions.

3. Layer quilt top, batting, and quilt backing. Baste. See Layering and Basting Quilts and Projects (page 137).

4. With the machine set for free-motion quilting, stitch a leaf design on each appliqué. Go over each line twice for a sketchy look. Use a dark thread for this step.

5. Using a thread that blends with the quilt top, quilt the remainder of the quilt top.

6. Bind. See Binding a Finished Quilt (page 138).

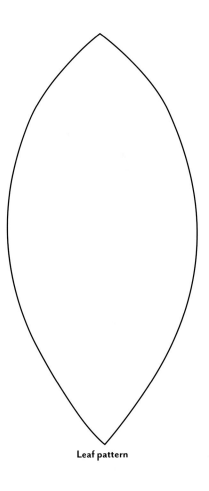

Leaf pattern

EMBROIDERED PROJECTS

When you're feeling comfortable, try stitching something without batting. It takes a little adjustment to stitch on a different "canvas," but it's definitely worthwhile! These projects involve simple construction or are stitched on purchased items for extra speed.

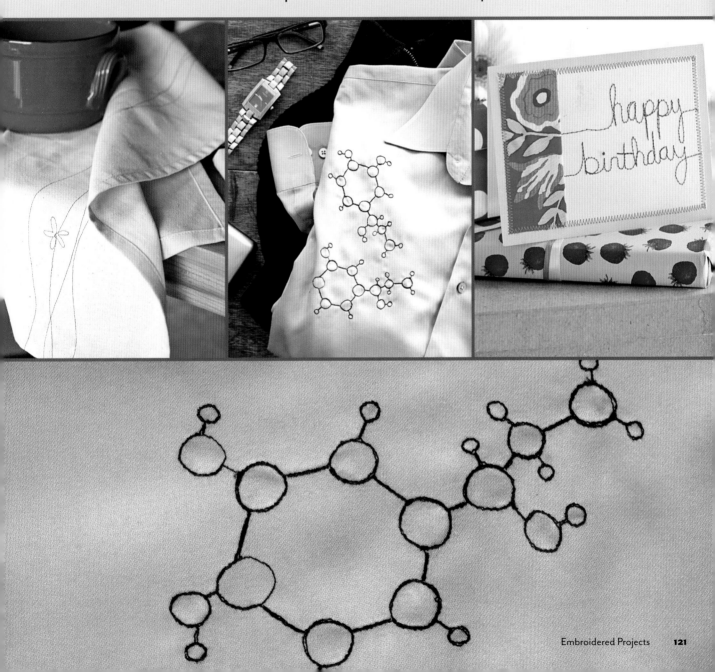

KITCHEN TOWELS

Finished size: Set of 2 towels, 16″ × 30″ each
Experience level: Getting it
Quilting design: Edge-to-edge lines

Prehemmed toweling makes this a quick project. You simply stitch the design and then finish the top and bottom edges! If you have a set of plain kitchen towels, you could stitch on those instead.

MATERIALS

Prehemmed toweling, 16″ wide: 2 yards

Spray starch

MAKE IT

1. Press the toweling twice with spray starch to provide stability while quilting.

2. Cut 2 pieces 32″ long from the toweling. Use the remaining piece of toweling to test the machine's tension settings.

3. With the machine set for free-motion work, quilt design on towels.

4. Press raw edges ½″ toward the back. Fold over another ½″ and press, so that the raw edge is concealed, and then pin. With the machine set for straight stitching, topstitch with thread that matches the toweling.

TIPS FOR STITCHING THIS PROJECT

- Start by stitching two gentle, wavy lines without flowers. Then stitch two wavy lines with a few flowers each. Let the lines occasionally overlap.

- Keep gentle outward pressure on the fabric while stitching to avoid puckering on the towels.

SCISSOR SKIRT

Experience level: Getting it
Quilting design: Sketching

What better way to declare your crafty nature? Free-motion stitching makes store-bought clothing much more interesting!

MATERIALS

Store-bought skirt

Wash-Away Stitch Stabilizer (by C&T Publishing) or transparent wash-away stabilizer

Paper water-soluble stabilizer or tear-away stabilizer

Fine-tipped permanent marker

MAKE IT

1. Copy the design onto the Wash-Away Stitch Stabilizer using an inkjet printer or trace onto transparent wash-away stabilizer.

2. Choose where you would like the design. Stick the adhesive-backed Wash-Away Stitch Stabilizer with the design on top of the area to be stitched and pin the bottom stabilizer to the wrong side of the fabric underneath the area to be stitched.

3. With the machine set for free-motion work, stitch over the stabilizer, following the design. Remove stabilizers according to the manufacturer's directions.

TIPS FOR STITCHING THIS PROJECT

- Trace the outline of the design once; then go around again and add the details inside.

- Don't worry about getting the second pass directly on top of the first. Slight variations give an impromptu, sketchy quality to the design.

- If you have some material similar to the skirt, practice stitching with stabilizers on it to check whether you need to adjust the thread tension. See Using Stabilizers (page 134).

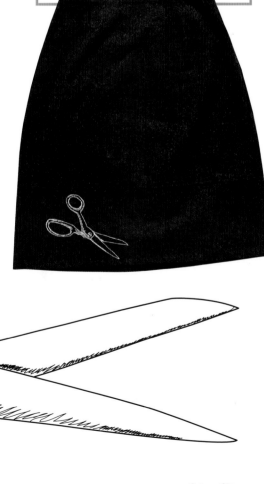

Scissor design

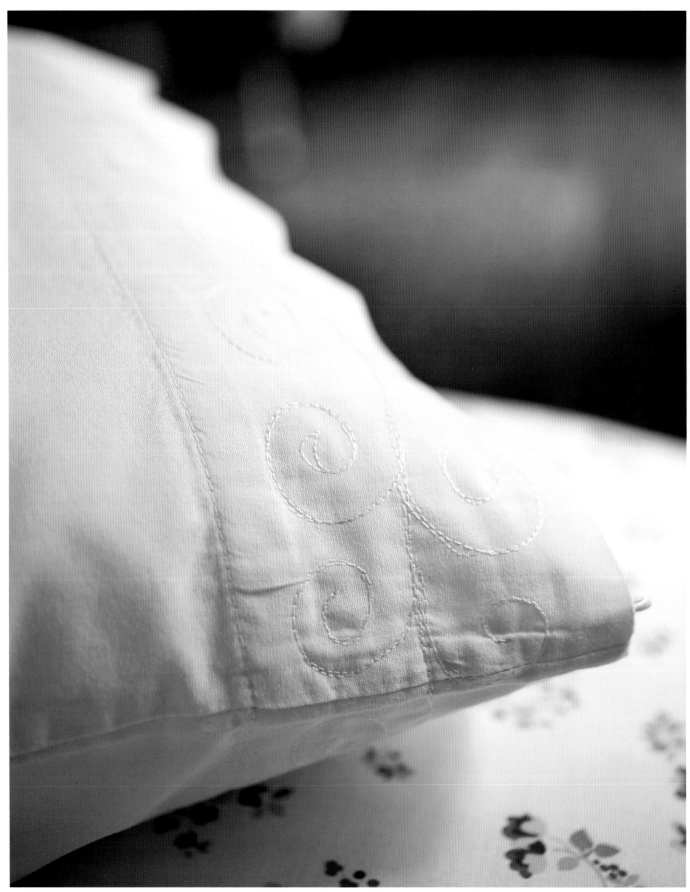

SPIRAL PILLOWCASES

Experience level: Comfortable
Quilting design: Spirals

This is a simple way to add a handmade touch to bedding.

MATERIALS

Store-bought pillowcases

Spray starch

MAKE IT

1. Prewash pillowcases to preshrink them. Press the pillowcase edges twice with spray starch to provide stability during stitching.

2. With the machine set for free-motion work, start by stitching a gentle wavy line around the entire circumference of the pillowcases.

3. After coming back to the beginning of the wavy line, begin adding spirals on either side of the wavy line.

TIPS FOR STITCHING THIS PROJECT

- The skinny area you are stitching can be hard to hold. Try grasping the fabric with one hand in front of and to the right of the needle, and the other hand in back of and to the left of the needle.

- Make sure not to stitch the pillowcase edges together!

ADRENALINE MOLECULE SHIRT

Experience level: Comfortable

Quilting design: Sketching

A simple design makes a purchased shirt one of a kind. Do you know any adrenaline junkies?

MATERIALS

Store-bought, button-down shirt

Spray starch

Wash-Away Stitch Stabilizer (by C&T Publishing) or transparent wash-away stabilizer

Paper water-soluble stabilizer

Fine-tipped permanent marker

MAKE IT

1. Press the area that will be stitched with spray starch.

2. Trace 2 copies of the design onto the Wash-Away Stitch Stabilizer using the permanent marker. Cut them out separately so they can be arranged as you wish.

3. Choose where you would like the 2 designs to be placed. Stick the 2 adhesive-backed Wash-Away Stitch Stabilizer pieces on top of the shirt, and pin the bottom stabilizer underneath on the wrong side of the fabric.

4. With the machine set for free-motion work, stitch over the stabilizer, following the design.

5. Remove stabilizers according to the manufacturer's directions.

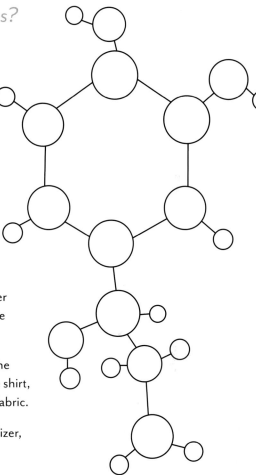

Molecule design

TIPS FOR STITCHING THIS PROJECT

- Stitch over every line at least twice to give the stitching visual weight.

- Go slow for precision. See Using Stabilizers (page 134).

BRANCHY SCARF

Finished size: 8¾″ × 62″ (The length is approximate and will depend on the width of the knit fabric used.)

Experience level: Comfortable

Quilting design: Sketching

A little free-motion embroidery makes a knit scarf even more delightful.

MATERIALS

Lightweight knit jersey: ½ yard

Wash-Away Stitch Stabilizer (by C&T Publishing) or transparent water-soluble stabilizer

Paper water-soluble stabilizer

Permanent marker

MAKE IT

1. Copy the design onto the Wash-Away Stitch Stabilizer using an inkjet printer or trace with the permanent marker.

2. Stick the adhesive-backed Wash-Away Stitch Stabilizer on top of the area to be stitched and pin the bottom stabilizer beneath the area on the wrong side of the fabric.

3. With the machine set for free-motion work, stitch the branches, following the design. Then change threads and add blossoms.

4. Clip the excess threads from between the blossoms. Remove the stabilizers according to the manufacturer's instructions. Allow the fabric to dry.

5. Fold the fabric in half lengthwise, right sides together, and pin. Sew along the 3 raw edges with a narrow zigzag stitch, leaving a 5″ opening along the long edge for turning.

6. Clip excess material at the corners and turn the scarf right side out. Hand stitch the opening closed. See Ladder Stitch (page 136).

TIPS FOR STITCHING THIS PROJECT

- Take several passes over the branches to fill them in and give a bark-like texture.

- While adding blossoms, you do not need to cut the thread between them. Just make sure you are taking a few close stitches at the beginning and end of each blossom to secure the threads.

Branch design

STITCHED CARD

Experience level: Comfortable
Quilting design: Words

Nothing beats being able to whip up a one-of-a-kind card from your sewing room. Why not have a small batch ready to go?

MATERIALS

Precut folded card   Fabric scrap   Rotary cutter

Card stock   Gluestick

MAKE IT

1. Start by stitching the message on the piece of card stock. I usually stitch the message several times on a full sheet until I get a version that I like.

2. Cut a rectangle with the stitched message from the card stock, at least ½" smaller in each direction than the front of the card.

TIP

A rotary cutter blade that is too dull for fabric will cut paper just fine!

----

3. Lay the scrap of fabric face down on the card stock. With the machine set for a straight stitch, sew a vertical line to attach the fabric to the card stock. Make sure you are stitching clear of the stitched words and that the fabric scrap will cover the card stock to the edge when turned over to the right side. Flip over and finger press the seam. Tack the fabric to the card stock with the gluestick so that it lies flat. Trim the fabric even with the edges of the card stock.

4. Tack the sewn card stock to the front of the card with the gluestick. Allow to dry. With the machine set for a zigzag stitch, sew the edges of the card stock to the card.

TIPS FOR STITCHING THIS PROJECT

- Stitching through paper requires a strong needle. If the needle seems to hesitate before piercing the paper, try a denim needle, which has less give to it.

- It takes a while to get a feel for working with paper. Expect that you'll waste a piece or two of card stock at the beginning.

- When you make a mistake, just stitch to the side an inch or two and start again.

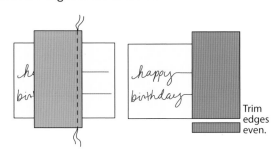

Trim edges even.

Sewing and Quilt Construction Techniques

SEAM ALLOWANCES

Unless otherwise noted, a ¼″ seam allowance is used for the projects in this book. I find my work looks best when seam allowances are pressed open. This makes for more consistent seam thickness and less chance that the darning foot will catch when I'm quilting over a seamline.

FABRIC MARKERS

While I don't premark quilting designs, I do find fabric markers very handy for project construction. Any temporary marker will do. Pencils, pen, and chalk all work well for the projects in this book. When possible, make the marks along the outside edge of the piece, within the area that will become the seam allowance. If the marks are in an area that will be visible in the completed item, test on a scrap first to make sure the marks are removable from the fabric you are using.

USING STABILIZERS

For some embroidery projects I recommend stabilizers. I use two different types:

Bottom stabilizers

These stabilizers provide a sturdy base for stitching that prevents puckering of the material from the thread tension. Pin the stabilizer on the wrong side of the fabric, underneath the area to be stitched. After stitching, remove the stabilizer according to the manufacturer's directions. The stabilizers I used for the projects in this book are Paper Solvy (wash away) and Tear-Easy (tear away).

Various stabilizers

Transparent (top) stabilizers

These stabilizers allow you to trace a design, stitch through it, and then wash away the stabilizer. Trace the desired design onto the stabilizer using a fine-tipped permanent marker. Pin the stabilizer to your work, stitch over the marked lines, and then remove the stabilizer according to the manufacturer's directions. The transparent stabilizers I used for the projects in this book are Super Solvy and Ultra Solvy, which are both wash-away stabilizers. I also recommend Wash-Away Stitch Stabilizer (by C&T Publishing), which is adhesive backed and doesn't require pinning.

FUSIBLE APPLIQUÉ

The appliqué projects in this book use lightweight fusible web for quick and easy appliqué. This web is a paper-backed, double-sided product that fuses two fabrics together. This method does not require adding a seam allowance. Trace and cut the pieces exactly as they are drawn. For the projects in this book I used Heat*n*Bond Lite.

1. Make a sturdy template for tracing the pattern. I make mine with a clear sheet of template plastic. Lay the template plastic over the appliqué pattern. Trace the pattern onto the plastic with a fine-tipped permanent marker. *(See Figure A.)* Cut out carefully along the marked lines.

Alternatively, you can make a template using a piece of thin cardboard, such as from a recycled food box. Glue a copy of the appliqué pattern onto the cardboard. Make sure the paper is glued flat. When dry, cut out carefully along the marked lines.

2. Cut a piece of fusible web the size directed in the pattern. Fuse to the back of the appliqué fabric. Make sure a bit of fabric extends beyond all edges of the fusible web, to avoid accidentally attaching the fusible web to the ironing board.

3. Trace around the template onto the paper of the fusible web as directed in the pattern. Cut shapes out along the traced lines. *(See Figure B.)*

4. Remove the paper backing from the web. Lay the appliqué pieces as desired on the background fabric. Pin in place if necessary. Use an iron to set the pieces according to the package instructions.

5. Secure the edges with a zigzag stitch if they will not be stitched during the quilting step. *(See Figure C.)*

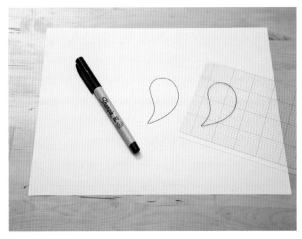

A.

B.

C.

BASTING PROJECT PIECES

To hold project pieces in place during construction, basting with thread or glue is sometimes helpful. Whether you use glue or thread, be sure to baste within the seam allowance so the basting will not be visible on the completed item.

To baste with glue, use a temporary fabric glue. A gluestick or plain white glue can be used as well. Apply a small amount of glue and allow pieces to dry before proceeding.

To baste with thread, use a long stitch length (four stitches per inch).

TOPSTITCHING

Topstitching lends a finished look to projects and can be used to close up holes that were left for turning. Stitch close to the edge with a straight stitch, using the presser foot as a guide. A topstitch needle will produce smoother stitching.

LADDER STITCH

A ladder stitch is a useful stitch for finishing a project so that the stitches do not show. It is used in this book to close up linings and the holes used for turning a project right side out.

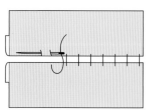

BOXING CORNERS

Boxing the corners of a sewn piece creates a three-dimensional bucket or bag with minimal work.

1. After sewing side and bottom seams, arrange and fold the corner of the piece so the side seam lies directly over the bottom seam. The corner will create a right angle. Pin in place if desired to avoid shifting. You may insert a pin through the middle of the top seam and make sure it emerges through the middle of the bottom seam to help with alignment.

2. Use a ruler to mark a stitching line perpendicular to the side seam. Place the line as needed to give the width recommended in the pattern.

3. Stitch along the marked line and trim away the excess corner, leaving a ¼″ seam allowance.

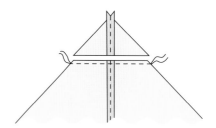

LAYERING AND BASTING
QUILTS AND PROJECTS

Layering and basting a quilt properly will prevent puckers as you stitch. When layering a quilt I make sure to give myself an extra 3″ of batting and backing on every side. This gives me plenty of space to place my hands and maneuver the quilt when stitching at the edges. For smaller pieces I make sure to have 1″–2″ of extra batting and backing extending beyond each edge.

To layer the quilt, spread the backing face down. If the piece is large, tape the edges down with masking tape. Make sure the fabric is taut but not stretched. (If you are working on carpet you can use sturdy pins to secure the backing to the carpet.) Center the batting on top, smoothing out any folds from the center to the edges. Place the quilt top right side up on top of the batting and backing, making sure it is centered. Smooth it out as flat as possible, from the center to the edges. Make sure you don't distort the quilt top.

Basting keeps the layers of the quilt sandwich from shifting while you are quilting. I use curved safety pins placed about 5″ apart across the quilt top. Be sure the pins go all the way through the backing fabric. Begin basting in the center and move toward the edges. To prevent shifting of the quilt as you work near the edges, you may place pins at the edges closer to each other, about 3″ apart.

BINDING A FINISHED QUILT

Trim excess batting and backing from the quilt even with the edges of the quilt top.

Cut the binding strips 2¼" wide and piece them together with diagonal seams to make a continuous binding strip. Trim the seam allowances to ¼". Press the seams open. *(See Figure D.)*

Press the entire strip in half lengthwise with wrong sides together. With raw edges even, pin the binding to the front edge of the quilt several inches away from a corner, and leave the first few inches of the binding unattached. Start sewing, using a ¼" seam allowance.

Stop ¼" away from the first corner *(See Figure E.)*, and backstitch a stitch. Lift the presser foot and needle. Rotate the quilt a quarter turn. Fold the binding at a right angle so it extends straight above the quilt and the fold forms a 45° angle in the corner. *(See Figure F.)* Then bring the binding strip down even with the edge of the quilt. *(See Figure G.)* Begin sewing at the folded edge. Repeat in the same manner at all corners.

Continue until you are back near the beginning of the binding strip. Join the ends using your preferred method, or do the following: Fold in the beginning tail of the binding strip ¼" so that the raw edge will be inside the binding after it is turned to the back side of the quilt. Place the end tail of the binding strip over the beginning folded end and trim to allow for a 1" overlap of the two ends. Continue to attach the binding and stitch slightly beyond the starting stitches. Fold the binding over the quilt's raw edges to the quilt back and hand stitch.

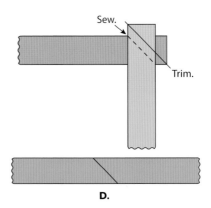

Sew.

Trim.

D.

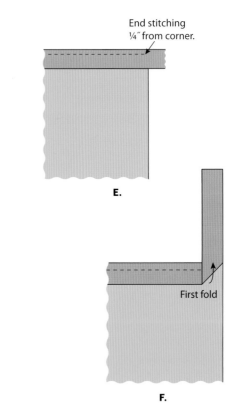

End stitching ¼" from corner.

E.

First fold

F.

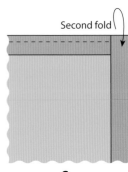

Second fold

G.

Troubleshooting

Little problems come and go with free-motion quilting. If you encounter a problem, work progressively through the lists below until you find the solution. While you're working through a problem, stitch on a practice pad. Go back to the project after you're certain you've solved the problem. You'll save yourself a lot of ripped stitches! Over time you'll learn your machine's temperament and navigating challenges like these will become second nature.

THREAD BREAKING

Is the machine skipping stitches before the thread breaks? If so, check out the next section.

- Take the spool off the machine and the bobbin out of the case, and then rethread the machine to make sure the bobbin is oriented correctly and the thread isn't wrapping around anything and catching.

- Try a different brand of thread. Choose one made for machine quilting to make sure it's not weak thread that's causing the problem.

- Try a different needle. If you're using an 80/12, try a 90/14. If you're using a 90/14, try a topstitch 90/14. If you are quilting through a tightly woven fabric such as batik, try a Microtex sharp needle. Make sure you are using a fresh needle.

- Is the top thread or bobbin thread tension too high? Try decreasing the tension on one or both threads. See Tension Adjustment (page 15).

- Be aware of pulling too hard on the quilt. Too much tension against the needle can cause thread to break. Make the quilting surface as smooth and flat as possible, and support the quilt so it doesn't hang off the table.

- Clean out lint from under the stitch plate and in the bobbin area.

- Are you pausing your hands while the machine continues to stitch? Repeated stitches in the same spot may cause the thread to break.

- Did you use a spray baste? If it is too thickly applied, spray baste can cause thread breakage.

- Inspect the entire thread path for a place where the thread might be catching. If a rough spot is causing the thread to catch, the sewing machine shop may be able to smooth it out.

SKIPPED STITCHES

When stitches are skipping, something is keeping the top thread from being in the right place to form a proper stitch.

- Rethread the top thread.

- Do a full lint cleanout under the stitch plate and in the bobbin area.

- Make sure you are using a fresh needle.

- Make sure the needle is large and sharp enough. Move up to an 80/12 or a 90/14. Try a Microtex sharp needle, particularly if you are quilting through a densely woven fabric such as batik or a bed sheet.

- Try a different thread. Many quilters report that their machines like certain brands of thread more than others.

- Try decreasing the top thread tension. Check the stitch tension on the back of your work. You may need to decrease the bobbin tension as well to compensate. See Tension Adjustment (page 15).

- Increase the pressure on the presser foot if your machine is able to adjust this setting.

- If you have been quilting with the feed dogs down, try leaving them up.

- Are you stitching through anything that could be grabbing the thread? The remaining wax on batiks or sticky fabric products can cause this problem. You may have better luck with polyester thread.

- Be aware of pulling too hard on the quilt. Too much tension against the needle can cause skipped stitches. Make the quilting surface as smooth and flat as possible, and support the quilt so it doesn't hang off the table.

- When was the last time your machine was serviced? The timing may need adjustment.

THREAD LOOPS ON THE BACK OF THE QUILT

- Make sure the presser foot is down. This is easy to forget! If you have lots of large hairy loops on the bottom, this is the most likely cause. Try again, double-checking that you've lowered the presser foot when you start stitching.

- Take the spool off the machine and the bobbin out of the case, and then rethread the machine. Make sure the presser foot is up when threading the top thread.

- Increase the top thread tension or decrease the bobbin tension. See Tension Adjustment (page 15).

- Are you moving your hands too fast? If you only see the loops when the stitches get long, it's because you need a more consistent stitch length. Keep practicing and try to move your hands a little slower or stitch a little faster. Pay special attention to curves: Practice keeping the stitching speed consistent as you go around them.

- Clean out the lint under the stitch plate and in the bobbin area.

- Try a different brand of thread. Many quilters report their machines like certain threads better than others. Make sure the top and bottom threads are the same weight or thickness.

- If you have been quilting with the feed dogs down, try leaving them up.

NEEDLE BREAKS

Needles tend to break when people are first learning to quilt. Hang in there!

- Are you moving the quilt too fast? Move your hands slower or speed up the stitching, or both.

- Take the spool off the machine and the bobbin out of the case, and then rethread the machine to make sure the bobbin is oriented correctly and the thread isn't wrapping around anything and catching.

- The thread tension may be too high. Decrease the top thread tension and recheck the stitches. You may need to decrease the top and bobbin tension together. See Tension Adjustment (page 15).

- Make sure the quilt is not hanging and putting too much stress on the needle. Support the quilt so it doesn't hang off the table.

- Are you quilting through something very dense, like denim or canvas? Try a denim needle.

BOBBIN THREAD SHOWING ON THE TOP

- Decrease the top thread tension. If the tension cannot be decreased, increase the bobbin thread tension slightly. See Tension Adjustment (page 15).

- Use a smaller needle.

- Use the same color thread in the bobbin as you do for the top thread. This won't solve the problem, but it will make it less noticeable.

THREAD SNARLS ON THE BACK OF THE QUILT

When it happens in the middle of stitching, thread snarls or birds' nests on the back side of the quilt are caused by the bobbin catching temporarily and then releasing and overspinning.

- If the problem is only happening at the beginning of the stitching, make sure you are bringing the bobbin thread to the top and holding on to the thread tails as you take the first stitches.

- Rethread the machine. Make sure the presser foot is raised as you thread the top thread.

- Do a full lint cleanout, paying special attention to the bobbin area. Check carefully for small collections of lint in the corners of the bobbin case.

- Try using the same thread in the top and the bobbin.

- Many newer machines have an anti-backlash spring to prevent bobbin overspin. If your machine's bobbin case does not have an anti-backlash spring in it, consider using a Teflon bobbin washer in the bobbin case. See Resources (page 143).

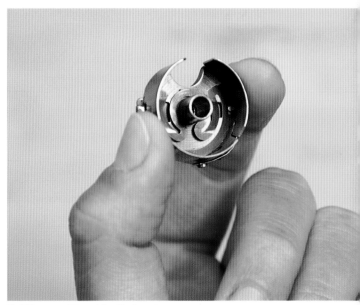

Bobbin case with anti-backlash spring

BUBBLES AND PUCKERS

As you quilt, you may notice that excess fabric is pushed around by the darning foot. When enough of this fullness accumulates, bubbles and puckers can form in the fabric.

- Try your best to accurately piece the quilt top so that it lies flat. Make sure it is freshly pressed when you layer it, and make sure you get the backing, batting, and quilt top as flat and smooth as possible when you baste.

- Make sure you are basting thoroughly. The more fullness you are dealing with in an area, the more the basting will matter. Keep the pins no more than 5″ apart. Place them even closer around the edges if the puckering tends to happen as you quilt the outer edges.

- Make sure the darning foot is not squishing the quilt sandwich. The darning foot should just brush the top of the quilt with the needle raised, allowing you to move the quilt freely. Reduce the pressure on the presser foot if your machine is able to adjust this setting.

- Make sure you are using the correct foot for your machine. Consult your local sewing machine shop to see if there is a better free-motion foot for your machine.

- Make sure you are applying slight downward and outward pressure with your hands as you stitch. This should help flatten the fabric in the area between your hands. You can also use your fingertips to guide the fabric bubble under the needle bit by bit as you work through the accumulated fullness.

- If your machine has a stitch plate that lifts above the feed dogs, or if you are using a detachable feed dog cover, try working without it (just set the machine's stitch length to zero).

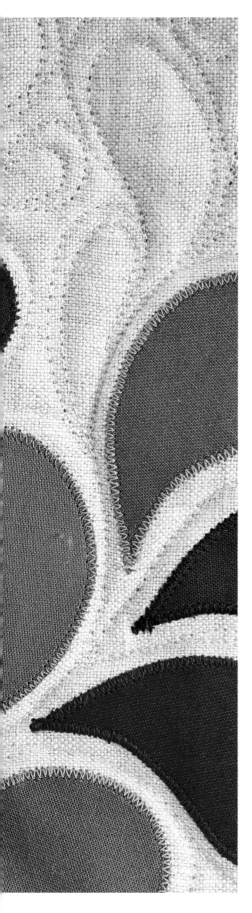

ABOUT THE AUTHOR

CHRISTINA CAMELI is a nurse-midwife and a quilter. She enjoys finishing quilts on her domestic machine and teaches free-motion quilting classes for beginners to help others do the same. She lives with her husband and children in Portland, Oregon, and shares her adventures in patchwork and quilting at afewscraps.blogspot.com.

RESOURCES

Stabilizers

Your local quilt shop is an excellent resource. In addition, try the following.

Wash-Away Stitch Stabilizer
ctpub.com

Sulky
sulky.com/stabilizers

Threads
Red Rock Threads
redrockthreads.com

Quilting/extension tables
Sew Steady
sewsteady.com

SewEzi
seweziusa.com

Quilting mats
SewSlip
sewslip.com

Supreme Free-Motion Slider
freemotionslider.com

Bobbin washers
Little Genie Magic Bobbin Washers
freemotionslider.com

Batting
Fabric Depot
fabricdepot.com

Template plastic for appliqué
Visi-GRID
ctpub.com